THE ARMOR OF GOD

PASTOR TYRANCE GREER

THE ARMOR OF GOD

XULON PRESS

Xulon Press
2301 Lucien Way #415
Maitland, FL 32751
407.339.4217
www.xulonpress.com

© 2019 by Pastor Tyrance Greer
Revised 2020

All rights reserved solely by the author. The author guarantees all contents are original and do not infringe upon the legal rights of any other person or work. No part of this book may be reproduced in any form without the permission of the author. The views expressed in this book are not necessarily those of the publisher.

Unless otherwise indicated, Scripture quotations taken from the King James Version (KJV)–*public domain.*

Scripture quotations taken from the Amplified Bible (AMP). Copyright © 1954, 1958, 1962, 1964, 1965, 1987 by The Lockman Foundation. Used by permission. All rights reserved.

Scripture quotations taken from the American Standard Version (ASV))–*public domain.*

Scripture quotations taken from the Holy Bible, New Living Translation (NLT). Copyright ©1996, 2004, 2007 by Tyndale House Foundation. Used by permission of Tyndale House Publishers, Inc.

Scripture quotations taken from the Holy Bible, New International Version (NIV). Copyright © 1973, 1978, 1984, 2011 by Biblica, Inc.™. Used by permission. All rights reserved.

Scripture quotations taken from the New King James Version (NKJV). Copyright © 1982 by Thomas Nelson, Inc. Used by permission. All rights reserved.

Printed in the United States of America.

ISBN-13: 978-1-5456-7565-6

TABLE OF CONTENTS

INTRODUCTION
ix

Chapter ONE
THE CORE
1

Chapter TWO
THE COVERING
15

Chapter THREE
THE CALL
39

Chapter FOUR
CONFIDENCE
51

Chapter FIVE
CONSCIOUSNESS
67

Chapter SIX
THE COMMISSIONING
83

INTRODUCTION

We live in a world where everything in life is not what it appears to be. There is more to life than what our eyes can see, as there are things that happen behind the scenes. There is another world that is hidden behind an invisible veil. Naturally, when we visit an ophthalmologist, our main objective is to identify if we have perfect vision, which is a perfect balance with both eyes. In the world of optometry, we know the phrase "20/20 vision." There is a natural side of things in life, and often our propensity is to believe what our eyes have beheld in the natural sense of life; this is the only source of reality to us, but before we were born, we had insight. According to Merriam Webster, the word "insight" means the power or act of seeing into a situation to apprehend the inner nature of things or the power or act of seeing intuitively. You had insight before you had eyesight. Without spiritual insight, this world will still go undetected.

When it comes to the spiritual side of life, the challenge with us is that we negate using spiritual truth, but why? We wrestle with the thought that unseen forces exist, but we will invest money in Hollywood movies that pertain to the supernatural side of life, such as X-Men, Thor, Avengers, and Endgame. In exercising our natural rights, we make what I consider our educational decision to select a fiction movie, but we have a real experience where we become emotionally unstable throughout the transition of the thoughts that the director has placed within the film. In this, we become open to the supernatural, and no one had to give us an elaborate thesis or a dissertation to get us to believe in what they introduced in society as fictional; society just believes.

With 20/20 vision, one side represents the natural side of life while the other represents the spiritual side of life, but they both work in harmony. If we are to see things as God sees them, there has to be a balance. We must view life from both perspectives, naturally and spiritually. We are in a war, and there is a spiritual terrorist camouflaging himself in his army fatigues, making an attempt to catch us off guard when we are fatigued (without strength). Satan's pedigree is to target families, communities, children, churches, and corporations. After he selects his victim, he stalks them, then he moves in for the kill by wreaking havoc on them.

The enemy tortures us with lies that he presents to us as God's truth. These lies only become relevant when we receive them as if they are real, and we are often stained by a thought that evades the memory banks of our mind. Torture is then initiated through meditation, the method that the enemy utilizes to take our strength. When our strength is no more, he leave us with scars of self-inflicted wounds. Who desires to live in a moment in their mind that they could never get past?

Are you walking around with your eyes wide shut? The phrase "eyes wide shut" means a person refuses to grasp life for how it really is, so the person could perhaps miss things that are hidden in plain sight. God's truth protrudes (sticks out) to

Introduction

supersede the enemy's lies; lies do not have the ability to live or exist in truth. This is why John 8:44 states that Satan is the father of lies. If he is the father of lies, why do we struggle with his information as truth? We often close our eyes because we are paralyzed in fear and pray that what has pierced our hearts is not the truth.

Cries rain out from our mothers and fathers when we become casual Christians, those who become complacent and compliant, losing sight of the danger that is at hand. When we become this, we will either be held captive (against our own will) or experience the casualties of war (death). Why? Because we have settled for convenience in critical moments. We are born-again Christians who are born for battle. We are warriors, and our destinies are won by a decision; however, without the proper perspective (understanding), we become paralyzed, mentally and physically, when we cannot spiritually penetrate the veil. The word "penetration" has multiple meanings; it is used in the context of intimacy, and Merriam-Webster defines the word "penetration" as discerning deeply and acutely. Until we can become intimate with God, we will not have the ability to discern deeply and acutely to move past the layers of natural reasoning to experience spiritual understanding. We allow ignorance to be an excuse for why the enemy is executing us, and we ending up being D.O.A. (Dead On Arrival).

We are in a war, and the battle is between the kingdom of darkness and the kingdom of light. This battle has always been over territory (land). In Genesis chapter one, when God created Adam, He formed him from the dust of the ground. Kings and kingdoms are governed by land, or territory. We are the children of the King of kings; we are His land, His territory, and the enemy desires to take authority over God's property. Land's

THE ARMOR OF GOD

greatest asset is that it can produce whatever you place in it. Similarly, whatever is sown into man, he becomes; this is why our nemesis desire us. However, when God finds the enemy trespassing on His property, He releases His angels, His chosen authoritative soldiers created for war, to evict the enemy off of His property. Every believer in Christ has a "No Trespassing" label upon his or her life. Isn't that amazing? Also, the acronym for "war" is:

Warriors
Able &
Ready.

This book was written from a biblical perspective, and the context was taken from the book of Ephesians chapter six, verse twelve. I am introducing this subject to enhance the spiritual awareness of readers who are interested in how different levels of prayer work and to expose how the kingdom of darkness functions. Battles are won and lost through either the right information or the lack thereof. Always remember, we never fight against flesh and blood (mankind), but our battle is against unseen forces that operate in darkness. This book is a guideline that will help you navigate through engaging in combat in the spiritual realm.

ARE YOU READY?

Chapter ONE

THE CORE

When you think about the core of anything, you think of the apex of why something exists. The core is the strength that maintains what surrounds the inside of any substance. To grasp a better understanding of a core, let's view a piece of fruit—a plum. The core of the plum is the seed, and the seed is the strength of the plum. Without the seed, there could not be any substance, or fruit. The fruit becomes the evidence that the seed existed; our success lives within the seed.

Another staggering thought is that the same seed that produced the plum matured into a tree. This is why it is befitting that the first part of God's armor He commands us to put on is the belt of truth. What is the purpose of a belt? Naturally, the purpose of a belt is to hold things in place; when you use a belt, you hold your garment in place so that you will expose your private place. Just as it is in the natural, so it is spiritually; the belt of truth covers and guards your private place, and the private places are the places where God has given us the ability to produce life. So the belt of truth will keep things in our lives in their proper places. Truth becomes the protective perimeter that will keep deceit out. A common example of this is when you "know" the truth of who you are, no one can convince you of who you are not. You cannot be of an Asian descent and have someone convince you that you are of an African descent. The truth about who you are or where you came from is revealed by a legal document—a birth certificate, which solidifies your birth. One truth that we have in life is we have a legal document (proof) that we can use to supersede every contradicting lie. What is that legal document for our faith? It is the Holy Bible, God's Word. There is a natural birth, and there is also a spiritual birth we find in Genesis 1:26 (NIV):

> [26] Then God said, "Let us make mankind in our image, in our likeness, so that they may rule over the fish in the sea and the birds in the sky, over the livestock and all the wild animals,[a] and over all the creatures that move along the ground."

Footnotes:

The Bible is the concrete evidence of where we came from and why we exist. I know we believe we have the chromosome from our mother or father, but our genetic structure didn't come from our forefathers. It was generated from our God, and the evidence in verse 26 explains how mankind came into fruition. A birth certificate identifies who our parents are, but the Bible is our legal, certified document to which we can refer or relate in times of uncertainty. No child is born without a birth certificate; neither is any child of God born again without their identification. Our birth certificate is the Bible.

The acronym for the word "Bible" is

Believers'
Instructional
Book for
Living
Every day.

God has given us an instruction manual that reveals how we were fashioned, where we came from, and how we are to function in life, our core. We were created from the hands of a Master Craftsman. We know Jesus by His earthly profession; He was a carpenter before His ministry started. Carpenters have an uncanny eye for paying attention to details. Their creativeness sets them apart from others, as they put things together in their minds before they ever assemble them with their hands. In John 1 (NIV), we read:

The Word Became Flesh

> **1** In the beginning was the Word, and the Word was with God, and the Word was God. ²He was with God in the beginning. ³Through him all things were made; without him nothing was made that has been made.⁴In him was life, and that life was the light of all mankind.

On earth, Jesus took the same role and position that He had in heaven. Another supporting verse brings even more insight. In Genesis 1:1-5 (ASV), we see how gracefully God created everything from the beginning:

In the beginning God created the heavens and the earth. And the earth was waste and void; and darkness was upon the face of the deep: and the Spirit of God [a]moved upon the face of the waters. And God said, Let there be light: and there was light. And God saw the light, that it was good: and God divided the light from the darkness. And God called the light Day, and the darkness he called Night. And there was evening and there was morning, one day.

God allows us to see how He thinks about situations, for we were born because there was a problem in the earth. This problem was that God's creation was incomplete; the earth was a desolate and uninhabitable place. The Bible gives us the connotation that God is a restorer, and He replenishes. He is a redeemer, and His thoughts reveal the blueprints of His mind, that He can take nothing and create something significant. God never agreed with His surroundings, so His surroundings became subject to what He thought.

Creative minds always find answers to problems that exist in life. Often it is the answers that lay dormant in us to society's problems, but it is also the problem that produces the thought so that the answer to society will emerge. The Master Craftsman, God, has assembled us with the solution. If things in our lives or society are coming apart, our responsibility is to go back and check the instruction manual, the Bible, which educates us on what steps to take. The Bible will show us how to put things in place. For example, one of the most essential parts of owning a new car is not only the keys but the instruction manual. The keys may give you access to turn on the vehicle, but can you move or operate a vehicle when you don't understand it? The instruction manual educates us on how everything works or functions, unless something on your car needs special attention. New cars have different functionalities: they have the ability to indicate when the oil needs to be changed, when the tire pressure is low, or when the car needs to be serviced. The problem with some car owners is they never invest time in reading the owner's manual, so when indicators in the car are revealed, they don't comprehend the signs that have been given to them. These are my questions to you: Are you experiencing complications? Has God been sending you signs and you are missing the information you are receiving because you never read the instruction manual (the Bible)?

One thing I have learned by purchasing new cars is that every car comes equipped with a manual. In faith, whether you are a newly converted Christian or you have been a part of the body of Christ for years, the Bible is the key to functioning in this vehicle called life. Cars have manufacturers, and when there is a recall, the manufacturer requires you to bring the car back to the dealership to replace the defective parts. If you feel that there is a defective area in your life, recall God by crying out to Him again, and He will give the authorization for you to come back to the manufactory. You may ask what the manufactory is; the manufactory is not a factory, but the manufacturer for the body of Christ is Jesus, the God that created mankind. When cars come off the assembly line, they are equipped with everything they need to function. When God created you, you were fully loaded; you have everything you need to be successful in life.

2 Peter 1:3 (KJV) states that "his divine power hath given unto us all things that pertain unto life and godliness."

The Bible helps us assemble our lives, step by step, in truth, so we will not establish our lives on the foundation of erroneous information: **lies**. As believers of Jesus Christ, we need to follow the instructions given to us for living on the earth; falling short or failure will only take place when we refuse to follow these instructions. In life, one of the greatest struggles we experience as believers is most of us grew up believing a façade. Satan specializes in optical illusions that appear to be real; this is Satan's pedigree. According to the latter part of John 8:44 (KJV), Satan is a liar and the father of lies.

Fathers have the potential to carry seeds that bring forth life. When seeds are planted, they will produce evidence that a father exists. Without a seed (child), a father cannot leave his legacy, for legacy can only live after the seed exists. Our children pick up the baton to continue the race and finish their part, and they must run with the same passion, focus, and authority. Children become the proof that we have the legal right on the earth to carry the title of father.

Satan's objective is to plant his seeds, his lies, which don't become realities until they have places to live. If we allow his seeds to germinate in our lives, then we give him the legal right on the earth to become a father, because when his seeds are planted, they manifest within our minds. Satan does not have a body, but his intention is for us to be his surrogate producers so that we may produce his offspring. Everything that comes into the earth realm only comes as a result of a believer. In order for conception to take place, there must be a time of ovulation. A normal pregnancy is not established until ovulation takes place, so Satan waits until we are at our time of fertilization. Why? Because that is the time when we can produce. In the book of Genesis, Adam and Eve were ovulated, and Satan sowed one seed into Eve. She carried his seed, the seed of disobedience, and it eventually established a generational curse; her firstborn son, Cain, carried the characteristic of Satan. Likewise, we are ovulated ground, and yielding to the enemy's tactics will give him the legal right on the earth to carry the title of father.

Fathers need sons to carry on their linage, so without us, he does not have a linage. This is why we must guard our hearts and minds, for whatever we think or feel, we become. The danger is that when our minds are not yielded to Jesus Christ, we will produce the wrong results. Satan's strategy is to get us to believe in his results. The acronym that we will use for the word "result" is:

Real

Exaggerated

Signs

Under

Life's

Test.

John 8:31-32 (KJV):

> Then said Jesus to those Jews which believed on him, if ye continue in my word, then are ye my disciples indeed; and ye shall know the truth, and the truth shall make you free.

According to the Scriptures, the reason the enemy fights us so intensely is because the truth shall make us free. So the ideology behind Satan's plans is to keep us in a place where we never feel free, mentally, financially, relationally, spiritually, and physically. The importance of your life will be predicated on the stability of your mind. That is why world wars take place. Repetitive thoughts that are established in your sub-consciousness are asking you for permission to live. There is a phrase that states seeing is believing; what we see in the natural was imbedded within the memory bank of someone's mind. The body will only react to what a person believes. I will express it from this perspective: If you desire to become a doctor, the mind needs something to meditate on, so the longer you meditate upon this desire, the stronger this desire will become. After the mind is made up, the body will soon follow; outer action is a result of inner belief. The mind is the most powerful tool we possess. Whatever you are passionate about, you will pursue; your pursuit is the evidence that a seed was planted. Whatever has been planted in you becomes your truth, and your truth will give birth to what you believe. Real truth is knowing Jesus Christ, for He is the truth, the way, and the life.

In Hebrew, the word "know" gives us the connotation of being intimate with God, not in a sensual way, but to connect with Him in a spiritual merging. According to Webster, in corporate America, the word "merger" means an agreement that unites two existing companies into one company. To know Jesus only means that you have come into agreement with Him because you have believed in Him. When there is a merger in business, both companies assume the same name. When you merge with Christ, you take His name, and that name gives you access to operate on the earth as He did. This is the power of attorney—when we experience the fullness of who He is and who we are in Him.

God left heaven, a perfect place of habitation, to be with us. Heaven is a place where there is no chronological time; if there is no time, just imagine worship happening continually. One of the reasons He left heaven was to teach us how to tabernacle (the word tabernacle means meeting place). In 1 Corinthians 6:19-20 (NIV), God's Word tells us:

> [19] Do you not know that your bodies are temples of the Holy Spirit, who is in you, whom you have received from God?

The place where God meets us is not outside of us; it is within us. Where there is an absence of truth (Christ), we leave atmospheric precipitation. Precipitation naturally brings out vapors that ultimately produce rain, hail, or snow. Satan desires to become our meteorologist so that he can change our atmosphere at home, at work, and with our children. Satan is the prince of the power of the air; he wants to control our environment and bring rain on our sunny days, according to Ephesians 2:2 (KJV):

> [2] Wherein in time past ye walked according to the course of this world, according to the prince of the power of the air, the spirit that now worketh in the children of disobedience:

Satan wants to produce his distorted truths. One thing we have learned in the court of law is that truth becomes the conclusive evidence that sets people free. Also, accusations are permitted in court, but without evidence, many cases that the accuser (Satan) has presented before God about us are not permissible in the courtroom of heaven. Many of us have never received the memo from heaven that our case, meaning our trial, was a mistrial.

Satan never had enough evidence to support his case. Based on our judicial system in America, when you cannot prove your case with concrete evidence, the judge dismisses the case and the one that was accused is set free. Jesus is our attorney, and He presented all the evidence that we will ever need to solidify our cases. He presented His body as the evidence to the judge, which happened to be His Father. The enemy attempted to present a picture of you, but Jesus presented the entire vision for you. His lies could not coexist with God's truth. When everything else fails, truth stands on its own. Oppositions are only opportunities for us to stand in faith until we see the results of truth.

The belt of truth is designed so that nothing is too large or too small for it. Truly, with this belt, one size does actually fit all: all colors, all creeds, and all cultures. So don't allow society to advert your attention away from the belt of truth, which is Jesus Christ. The belt is centered around our core; our core is our midsection, which is our place of strength. If the enemy can attack your core, he has the ability to take your strength. Have you ever been hit below your belt? If so, often if your core is not developed, one blow can take the wind right out of you. In the same way, if we never develop a relationship with Jesus, the enemy can sucker punch us and take us away from the truth—Jesus Christ. God's intention was for us to surround ourselves with Him, for He is the core, the strength of our existence.

Say these prayers with intensity and with authority!

1). I command every spirit of lies and deception coming against my bloodline to collide with the spirit of truth, in the name of Jesus.
2). I bring to bay every evil power of distortion trying to govern my thoughts and imagination, in the name of Jesus.
3). Let every manipulating, mind-hindering spirit be banished from my life, with chains and fetters of iron that can never be broken, in the name of Jesus.
4). I destroy and disgrace all destiny-aborting spirits, in the name of Jesus.
5). By the power of the blood of Jesus, let any cerebrospinal fluid leaking from my brain receive restoration, in the name of Jesus.
6). I bind and rebuke neurological disorders and diseases, in the name of Jesus.
7). I release myself from every inherited bondage, in the name of Jesus.
8). Let every power clinging to life and destiny be extinct, in the name of Jesus.
9). Let every demonic census trying to use my mind against God die, in the name of Jesus.
10). Heavenly Father, let Your indictment be placed upon every evil power trying to provoke my mind into corruption, in the name of Jesus.
11). We decree and declare destruction upon every telepathic and psychic power seeking to pollute and steal our thoughts, in the name of Jesus.

THE ARMOR OF GOD

12). Let whirlwinds and disasters take place in the camp of every enemy coming against my mental stability, in the name of Jesus.

13). I command dementia, Alzheimer's, Parkinson's, and Huntington disease and disorder to be degenerated, in the name of Jesus.

14). Every gallows of Haman constructed for my life, let that noose come around his or her neck and let it be his or her own demise, in the name of Jesus.

15). I renounce and denounce every reproach of Egypt off my life, in the name of Jesus.

16). Let the angel of the Lord destroy every demonic hunter desiring my life, in the name of Jesus.

17). I cover the gates of mind with the blood of Jesus from satanic and demonic subliminal messages, in the name of Jesus.

18). Father, remove the scales from my mind and enlighten the eyes of my understanding, in the name of Jesus.

19). All secret and hidden curses operating in my bloodline against my life and destiny dry up at the roots, in the name of Jesus.

20). Father, destroy every banshee spirit wailing against my life. I crush their vocal cords; destruction shall not come near my borders, in the name of Jesus.

21). For satanic particles that have been released into my body through food, let the blood of Jesus cleanse every organ from toxics and poisons, in the name of Jesus.

22). Every evil cloud hovering over my life, vanish, in the name of Jesus.

23). Satanic powers delaying my breakthroughs, be dispersed, in the name of Jesus.

The Core

24). Let the hammer of the Lord crush every tarantula seeking to entangle and devour my life, in the name of Jesus.

25). I decree and declare every small fox trying to destroy the vine of my life to receive devastation, in the name of Jesus.

26). Lord, decapitate every antagonizing spirit; smite them with madness and blindness, in the name of Jesus.

27). Let every witchcraft coven gathered against me be obliterated, in the name of Jesus.

28). Every evil practitioner pronouncing curses against my life be utterly destroyed, in the name of Jesus.

29). I break the teeth of every vampire spirit that seeks to drink our blood. My blood shall be poison to you, in the name of Jesus.

30). Let every hijacking spirit seeking to steal my blessing be dismantled, in the name of Jesus.

31). Witch and warlock powers commissioning darkness against my life receive fire, coal, and brimstone, in the name of Jesus.

32). Let the fire of God consume every web of deception in my life, in the name of Jesus.

33). Father, let every satanic cobweb in my life be cast down, in the name of Jesus.

34). Let every venomous black widow and brown recluse spider trying to release venom into my life wage war against your senders, in the name of Jesus.

35). Let every boasting Goliath threatening my life receive the anvil of the Lord, in the name of Jesus.

Chapter TWO

THE COVERING

Genesis 1:26 (KJV)

And God said, Let us make man in our image, after our likeness: and let them have dominion over the fish of the sea, and over the fowl of the air, and over the cattle, and over all the earth, and over every creeping thing that creeps upon the earth.

Adam was the first man God created, and this is the first time that we see our Creator God create a duplicate. When God created mankind, He made His mirror image, and mirrors only reflect the image that is placed before them. Adam didn't have an identity; he was never in need of one. When we take on an identity, we only do so because we have separated ourselves from God. Reputations are only for recognition, but when we are recognized by man, we lose the relationship with God. Reputations have to be built, but in building yourself up, ask yourself, "What or who have I torn down?" The first man, Adam, carried the image and likeness of God, and he had a protective covering—the glory of God. This covering could not be penetrated. When God makes investments in His people, He will always look for a return. To give us a more relevant view, we see this protective covering in Job 1:10 (NIV):

> [10] Have you not put a hedge around him and his household and everything he has? You have blessed the work of his hands, so that his flocks and herds are spread throughout the land.

Within the perimeters of Adam's life, there was no place of weakness that an enemy could penetrate; his relationship with God was beautiful, and his love was the barricade that could not be broken. When we love God, our fortress can never be broken; I am not referencing an outer fortress. Brokenness does not come from being broke (without financial stability); brokenness comes when we are broken. Before Adam failed his assignment, his armor was impenetrable; nothing could penetrate it until a mistake took place. Mistakes establish moments in which demarcation creates monuments of failure. Demarcation only sets up boundaries and limits, and religion becomes the opium that places a wedge between you and God. God does have a limit, but we just limit Him based on the condition of our mind. Conditions don't change God; God changes condition. He can change our surroundings, but He never impedes upon the obstruction of our thought life. He gives us the time and space to make a decision.

When Adam was in unity with God, God brought the animals to Adam. In Genesis 2:19 (NIV), we read:

¹⁹ Now the LORD God had formed out of the ground all the wild animals and all the birds in the sky. He brought them to the man to see what he would name them; and whatever the man called each living creature, that was its name.

Decisions mark our level of maturity, and like any father, God will stand abroad to see the maturity of His child. God allowed Adam to make the decisions to name all of the animals. God was so proud of the decisions Adam made that He allowed him to name his soulmate. God agreed with Adam because there was no disagreement within Adam. One thing the enemy hates is unity, and where you find unity, you will always find harmony. In Genesis 3:6-7 (NIV), we learn:

⁶ When the woman saw that the fruit of the tree was good for food and pleasing to the eye, and also desirable for gaining wisdom, she took some and ate it. She also gave some to her husband, who was with her, and he ate it. ⁷ Then the eyes of both of them were opened, and they realized they were naked; so they sewed fig leaves together and made coverings for themselves.

A landmark was placed in history where mankind had fallen. Adam and Eve were victorious until they removed their helmet and their minds were penetrated. You are inwardly as strong as your mind, so when their minds were penetrated, they became vulnerable. The end result of their failure was that they became victims, for they didn't obey God and lost their protective covering. This was the first time that Adam and Eve had seen themselves (their flesh), as the armor and the hedge was lifted. They lost their abilities to withstand an attack. All of mankind is still suffering from the mistake that Adam and Eve, our ancestors, made; their lack of obedience made us venerable and subjected to attacks. We have a nemesis, an archenemy, named Satan, who knows all about covering, as shown in Ezekiel 28:12-15 (KJV):

> Son of man, take up a lamentation for the king of Tyre, and say to him, "Thus says the Lord God: 'You were the seal of perfection, Full of wisdom and perfect in beauty.
>
> 'You were in Eden, the garden of God; every precious stone was your covering: The Sardis, topaz, and diamond, Beryl, onyx, and jasper, Sapphire, turquoise, and emerald with gold. The workmanship of your timbrels and pipes was prepared for you on the day you were created.
>
> 'You were the anointed cherub who covers; I established you; You were on the holy mountain of God; you walked back and forth in the midst of fiery stones.
>
> You were perfect in your ways from the day you were created, till iniquity was found in you.'"

When we look at the above scripture, we find Lucifer's covering in the beginning was made of precious stones, but it didn't matter how precious the stones were; it wasn't glory. Rather, the radiance from God's glory caused Lucifer's jewels to shine. Jewels don't shine until some form of light is cast upon them. Mankind reflected the radiance of God, but Lucifer lost his covering; his intention turned quickly toward mankind. God gave mankind what Lucifer desired: His radiances, authority, dominion, image, and likeness. When we reflected God's image, Satan became jealous, and jealousy breathed contempt.

Satan deceived Adam and Eve, and they removed their breastplates of righteousness to where the enemy infiltrated their hearts. The most intricate part of the breastplate of righteousness is what lies beneath it: the heart. It is our hearts that keep us in righteous standing with God.

One of the greatest misconceptions in the body of Christ is that we often fail to comprehend that we are in a war. In Hosea 4:6 (KJV), God says, "My people are destroyed for the lack of knowledge." It appears that we have centered our attention on gifts and talents instead of knowledge, although gifts and talents play their part in the body of Christ. But if we only focus our attention on those areas alone, we will never have the ability to be attentive, to be aware, and to be watchful when an attack comes. When your eyes do not have a propensity to stay open in war, eventually, the shutters of life (your eyes) will permanently be closed, and your life source (your spirit) will return back to its source.

One of the greatest lines of defense for the believers in Christ is their protective covering, but oftentimes, as believers, we are unaware that God has equipped us with armor. Armor was never created for fashion; armor was designed for protection and for engaging in war (combat). No one is issued armor without first being enlisted in an army. We are God's tactical team, His combat strategists for battle. Armor without blemishes or marks indicates that the soldier never engaged in warfare for his or her assignment. In 1 Samuel 17:13 (KJV), the Scriptures tell us:

And the three eldest sons of Jesse went and followed Saul to the battle: and the names of his three sons that went to the battle were Eliab the firstborn, and next unto him Abinadab, and the third Shammah.

In this passage of Scripture, we find that Eliab, Abinadab, and Shammah, David's older brothers, were following King Saul for forty days and nights. They were dressed for the occasion but not prepared to fight. In the body of Christ, the problem that we are faced with is that we are dressed for the occasion (church), and we look good in our outward adornments (clothing) at church, but our fine knits and clothing don't prepare us for battle. David's brothers proved that they could follow the king (Saul), but they didn't have the intestinal fortitude to fight for him. The issue here is that they were under a leader who lost his anointing to fight, which we find in Isaiah 10:27 (KJV):

And his yoke shall be destroyed because of the anointing.

Without the anointing, nothing can be destroyed. Where there is an absence of the anointing, there is an absence of God's presence. In Psalm 133:2 (NASB), the passage describes the precious oil upon the head coming down upon the beard, even Aaron's beard, coming upon the edge of his robes. From a natural perspective, we get oil from an olive, but olives are seasonal and must be selected at the right time. After they are selected, they are crushed for the purpose of the oil. Oil is a lubricant, and without lubrication in our life, we will eventually become dry, brittle, and useless. The anointing had a cost; can we pay the cost to carry it? God waits until we come into a mature state to measure the oil that is released from heaven onto our life. The anointing flows down from the head, and the head is Christ. Then Christ pours out His anointing upon the leaders and every other person within God's military platoon. We receive the anointing as long as we are in line with God and in agreement with Him. 1 Samuel 16:14 tells us that an evil spirit came upon Saul, and when David played his instrument, the evil spirit left. But when David left the presence of Saul the king, the evil spirit resume his position and merged with Saul.

In Matthew 12:25, Jesus said that a house divided against itself cannot stand. If Saul was operating with an evil spirit from within, how could he defeat Goliath, when they were on the same team? Satan will never fight against someone within his own army, so it would be insane if he wouldn't only fight those that oppose him. As soldiers in the body of Christ, we represent Jesus, who happened to be the anointed one, whose oil or anointing would never run dry. So if we are submitted unto Him, how can we lose a battle, when you and God are the majority? You can only function in authority when you are under authority. Staying obedient to God's will causes demonic powers to obey you; this becomes the law of the seed. In Genesis 1:11 (KJV), God said:

> 11 And God said, Let the earth bring forth grass, the herb yielding seed, and the fruit tree yielding fruit after his kind, whose seed is in itself, upon the earth: and it was so.

Every seed will produce after its own kind. In this verse, God was not only referencing vegetation, but He was also including our deeds and actions. Naturally speaking, it doesn't make sense to follow the King of kings and Lord of lords but never have the courage to fight for Him. Many of God's chosen leaders in the body of Christ have become socialists because they have turned our churches into public forums that advocate socialism and address political theories and political policies more than the Word of God. We have allowed politicians to use God's church as a platform to promote their political views to get votes, and some preachers have stood by and watched them pollute God's holy place. We have entered into an era of making errors because we are stuck on teaching God's chosen people delusional practices and messages about prosperity. Even though I am a firm believer in prospering, we have preached to our congregation from one side of it to another, and we have not provided balance to present the message in its entirety.

We can argue about doctrine, about who was right and who was wrong, and we can have theological debates. But when you have evidence, you can drop the debate. When you listen to a leader's message and every message alludes to money, or they mention saving accounts more than saving souls, you are listening to an illusionist. An illusionist's objective is to perform tricks to deceive you, and, oftentimes, when he is finished, he makes your money disappear. The first sign of prosperity was when God breathed into man, and man became a living soul. In the King James Version, 3 John 1:2 states, "I wish above all things that you may prosper and be in health even as your soul prospers." The Word of God is the breath of God. The Word is the life source of heaven, for it enhances and empowers the soul. When God becomes your source of life, illusionists and puppeteers cannot deceive you with substitutes.

There is a term in the King James Version of the Bible that is used for the word prosperity: "spoils." To some believers, the word **"spoils"** is an ugly word. 1 Samuel 17:25 (KJV) says:

> ²⁵ And the men of Israel said, Have ye seen this man that is come up? surely to defy Israel is he come up: and it shall be, that the man who killeth him, the king will enrich him with great riches, and will give him his daughter, and make his father's house free in Israel.

In order to receive spoils, you had to defeat your enemies in battle. David enquired about what he would receive if he defeated Goliath; he wanted to know what the spoils for defeating God's enemies would be. I feel some believers have become spoiled rotten in the body of Christ. Why? Instead of being a sweet aroma, some of us have become a stench in the nostrils of our Heavenly Father. Why? We expect God to give us His favor when we never had the intention of fighting for His kingdom. God's problems still persist on the earth because He fights with us to become us. This terminology means that God is trying to get us to become who we already are. We need to take our rightful places and step into our roles while being mature. When maturity emerges, we will no longer fight against God; we will fight for Him. In the Scriptures, we find that David was just considered a young shepherd who was only sent as a delivery boy. His brothers considered him to be delusional because of his desire, but David was different. He only wanted what God desired. Desires will only manifest when we are disciplined, and it was David's discipline that birthed God's desire.

David moved out of spiritual impulse; however, when the favor of heaven is on your life, it will always initiate fights on earth. David's first fight came from his own family, and families without discernment only become pawns that the devil will use to try to destroy or derail you from your destiny. Your desire must be stronger than their devices. David's desire had to be stronger than his family. Ambitions, desires, and destinies go hand and hand. You can never reach your destiny without a desire, for desires become your lasso that you release to pull in your destiny. David used his lasso, his love for God, and pulled in what he was destined to be in life; he was born to be a champion. Without being technical, I will state that hell had selected its champion (Goliath), and heaven had selected its champion (David). The Bible said the battle was put in array.

1 Samuel 17:2 (KJV):

> ²And Saul and the men of Israel were gathered together, and pitched by the valley of Elah, and set the battle in array against the Philistines.

Champions are not chosen by height or stature, for David was selected because of his heart for God.

1 Samuel 16:6-7 (NLT)

> When they arrived, Samuel took one look at Eliab and thought, "Surely this is the Lord's anointed!"

> But the Lord said to Samuel, "Don't judge by his appearance or height, for I have rejected him. The Lord

doesn't see things the way you see them. People judge by outward appearance, but the LORD looks at the heart."

It is the first time that we get the opportunity to view how God selects kings for kingdoms. The king had to ultimately reflect the image and the likeness of God. What was the image and the likeness? His heart. God rebuked the prophet Samuel because his perception was about physical strength, not the spirit of God. In 1 Samuel 16:7, the Bible says that God rejected Eliab, David's oldest brother, for he never had the character to lead. We often naturally believe the façade that because a person is older or they have been in a position longer than us, they are mature, but that is not so. Some people's bodies will outgrow their minds. Don't be deceived by outward appearances when people can't manage their actions and attitudes. We cover who we expect to keep. My question is why do we put leaders in positions that God has rejected? Let's see why God rejected Eliab. God said Eliab was rejected because of his heart. We chose people based on accolades, which become the source of their strength. But when their strength runs out, eventually, so do they because they had natural strength. The natural fades, and when people lose it or blow up, we are left wounded from the shrapnel of their lives.

We find this truth again in the Scriptures through the story of Esau and Jacob and birthright, which was always given to the firstborn. However, God revealed to their mother that He was changing the ordinance in the earth and that the elder would serve the younger one. Why didn't God choose Esau? Genesis 25:23 (KJV) tells us:

²³ And the LORD said unto her, Two nations are in thy womb, and two manner of people shall be separated from thy bowels; and the one people shall be stronger than the other people; and the elder shall serve the younger.

Esau was a mighty hunter; he had an impeccable ability to trap and catch his prey. His strength was his natural instinct to hunt. Instinct relies on your skillset and your five senses, not on the Holy Spirit. The challenge with instinct is that it eventually runs out, or you will experience a bad day with instinct. So, when Esau's instinct (strength) failed him, he could not secure food for himself; he sold his birthright to his brother Jacob for a bowl of beans. Your heart will reveal where you really are in God; either you will be sold out for God or you will sell out for Satan.

God desired a new king, and time was of the essence, so God gave Samuel the kingdom mandate to go to Jesse's house. He instructed him on how to officiate the inauguration, and His instruction was to make a sacrifice. The new king's success came by way of sacrifice; something had to give up his or her life so the new king's throne would be established for the kingdom of God. God searched the land, not for a physical location, but He was searching the ground of men's hearts. God told Samuel, "I have concluded my search. I have found Me a man that is after My own heart."

1 Samuel 13:14 (KJV)

¹⁴ But now thy kingdom shall not continue: the LORD hath sought him a man after his own heart, and the LORD hath commanded him to be captain over his people,

because thou hast not kept that which the LORD commanded thee.

Saul, the former king, no longer had the rhythm of heaven; the heartbeat was irregular, and when we are not synchronized with heaven, Satan finds a way to sneak in. God is moved, and we must be sensitive to God so that we will know when He is moved.

1 Samuel 16:11 (NIV)

¹¹ So he asked Jesse, "Are these all the sons you have?"

"There is still the youngest," Jesse answered. "He is tending the sheep."

Samuel said, "Send for him; we will not sit down until he arrives."

At the time, David was not in his father's house, but he was in the field. When we read in the verse above, we see that Samuel stopped the processional and said that no one could sit until David, the last son, came in. It reminds me of when a judge steps into a courtroom and the officer states, "All rise." Notice the bailiff doesn't carry the authority to announce the judge. The one who announces the person in authority is the one who understands authority. In the court of law, everyone stands until further instruction is given, because it is a sign of honor and respect for the judge. Samuel was under the authority of God, and he made David's entire family honor and respect David because he was someone they never considered. God moved David out of the field he was working in and brought him back to his father's house.

When God chooses you, He will make sure you don't miss your moment. God will not allow people to rest and have comfort until you take your rightful position. He will take you out of the field that you are working in to present you to others who He has chosen. God's selection revealed who He rejected, because David had seven older brothers that passed before the prophet Samuel several times, but the oil of heaven was never released (1 Sam. 16:10 KJV). What was the secret, and why didn't the oil flow upon David's brothers? One of the mysteries lies within the horn of oil. The horn came from a ram, as rams only develop horns when they have come into a place of maturity. Oftentimes, a ram will lose its life for the price of its horns. Also, some people are not prepared to surrender their lives to carry the oil of heaven. David's brothers never crossed over into the place of spiritual adulthood, for God will not allow us to carry the kingship of heaven when we still function and live the life of an adolescent on the earth. The wrong action and attitude will give birth to disasters. Here, the oil represents lubrication; it is what keeps us from becoming dry, for dry things become brittle and crack without moisturizing.

If you view this with me from a natural perspective, we can gather and understand a spiritual truth in this illustration. In certain cultures, skin pigmentation requires regular moisturizing: without the skin staying moisturized, it will become flakey, cracked, and irritated. Medically, some studies and physicians have label this condition as eczema. According to yahoo.com, eczema is defined as symptoms including irritated or inflamed skin. Without God's anointing, we become people in the body of Christ that have not been lubricated with the oil of heaven and have developed a bad case of spiritual eczema. Whenever you find people that have not sacrificed their lives to carry the oil of heaven, they become irritated and their hearts are inflamed. Living sacrifices are people who have willingly surrendered their lives to carry God's purpose on the earth. The Bible reveals unto us a powerful truth: out of an entire nation, only one person, David, had the right heart to carry out God's assignment on the earth. Can God trust you with His purpose on earth?

Proverbs 4:23 (NLT)

Guard your heart above all else, for it determines the course of your life.

God allows us to be guardians of our destinies. Our destinies are governed by our stewardship, and God has charged us to be mangers of guarding our hearts against evil. Our hearts are the incubated grounds that bring forth transformation. If we are not careful and watchful, the enemy can come into the fertile places of our hearts and sow seeds of mayhem; God has reserved those places for Him to perform miracles. In life, if you are observant, you can find evidence of who is guiding a person's life; actions are always reflectors. According to Ephesians 5:1, if God is the source of our lives, we should be imitators of Christ and walk in love. Perception becomes reality, for who we imitate will only regulate our hearts. Naturally, when the heart fails, so does the life of the person. The heart is the life source that keeps the body functioning.

Prayer is the place of protection:

1). Let every wicked power that is trying to deceive me, to pollute my heart, be disgraced, in the name of Jesus.

2). Heavenly Father, heal and remove generational curses where our forefathers have allowed demonic powers to infect the grounds of our hearts, in the name of Jesus.

3). Let every evil flow that is circulating around our hearts that is drawing evil repercussions against me be cleansed with the blood of Jesus.

4). Let every heredity sickness involving heart issues that have been affecting my bloodline be healed, in the name of Jesus.

5). For every root of bitterness that is keeping anger alive in me and affecting my heart, let the evil roots wither and die, in the name of Jesus.

6). I break and destroy every evil soul-tie trying to recon nect and deceive my heart, in the name of Jesus.

7). I bind and rebuke every vindictive spirit seeking to gain an entrance to my heart, in the name of Jesus.

8). I command death and destruction against every familiar spirit operating in my life, in the name of Jesus.

9). Holy Spirt, cleanse any parts of my heart that are not pleasing unto God, in the name of Jesus.

10). I cancel every spirit of death and defeat that has been hiding in my life. I command that you receive double destruction, in the name of Jesus (Jer. 17:18).

11). I close every revolving door of disappointment and setback that has been functional in my life, in the name of Jesus.

12). Let the wicked host of hell holding up my blessing, trying to make my heart sick, be dispersed, in the name of Jesus.

13). I bind and rebuke every witch and warlock speaking perpetual curses against my heart for it to fail, in the name of Jesus.

14). Let every demonic serpent twisting and coiling around my heart to squeeze the life out of me die, in the name of Jesus.

15). Let every evil acupuncturist trying to withdraw virtue from my life receive madness and blindness, in the name of Jesus.

16). For every satanic whisper, whispering evil séances against my life, let the hand of the Lord crush your larynx, in the name of Jesus.

17). For the witches that have gathered and assembled themselves around a caldron pot, summoning evil against my day, let their curses come upon them, in the name of Jesus.

18). Let every tarantula that is spinning webs for my life and family be paralyzed, in the name of Jesus.

THE ARMOR OF GOD

19). I decree and declare every spirit of distraction to be extracted from my life, in the name of Jesus.

20). Let the spirit of Jezebel hunting down my life receive defenestration from the spirit of Jehu, in the name of Jesus.

21). For the spirt of Athaliah that is seeking to destroy kids before they take their kingship, I release the executioner of heaven upon you, in the name of Jesus.

23). Father, destroy every demonic king that is trying to sit on the throne of my life, in the name of Jesus.

24). For the spirit of Herodias that has issued a warrant for my head, let the same axe that has been issued to kill me decapitate her head from her body, in the name of Jesus (Mark 6:24).

25). I raise up a voice of repentance for this nation; Father, forgive us for martyring innocent lives in this country, in the name of Jesus.

26). Father, reverse every evil curse that has come upon this nation because of the blood that has been spilled and is crying out for justice in the land, in the name of Jesus.

27). Let every prostituting spirit of Tamar looking to enslave our leaders with demonic deception die, in the name of Jesus (Gen. 38:13-15).

28). Let every satanic and demonic interference delaying our promotion and breakthroughs have the axe of the Lord sever them, in the name of Jesus.

29). I discombobulate those that are conspiring evil conspiracies against my life and family, in the name of Jesus.

30). I bind and rebuke every compromising spirit that has called the body of Christ to stumble and fall, in the name of Jesus.

31). I destroy and disgrace every spirt of mammon that has entered into our sanctuaries and polluted the holy place, in the name of Jesus.

32). I dismantle every spirit of discord roaming through our sanctuaries, in the name of Jesus.

33). Let every secret and hidden parishioner of Satan disguising themselves as ministers of the gospel in our congregation be exposed and perish, in the name of Jesus.

34). Let every evil cyclone and whirlwind that has been sent against my house and family be rerouted back to its senders, in the name of Jesus.

35). I revoke every evil contract with my name and my address on it, in the name of Jesus.

36). Let every evil fetter of religion that has held me captive be broken off of my life, in the name of Jesus.

37). I send chaos and devastation into demonic concentration camps, against demonic powers holding God's people hostage, in the name of Jesus.

38). I decree and declare that the fear of the Lord will fall upon every witch doctor conjuring evil potion against me, in the name of Jesus.

40). Father, let there be a dismantling of every demonic hunter that is seeking my life. Let the angels of the Lord hew them down and let none escape, in the name of Jesus.

41). Let the spirit of misery that is trying to bring distress and discomfort to my mind and my body be utterly destroyed, in the name of Jesus.

42). For every demonic power trying to bring an outbreak of malaria upon the life of any believer, I foil your plans and plots so they are frustrated, in the name of Jesus.

43). Let the healing virtue of the blood of Jesus restore healing and health to every malfunctioning organ in my body, in the name of Jesus.

44). I command every contentious spirit that is causing slipped discs and hernias to wage a war against itself and leave our bodies and self-destruct, in the name of Jesus.

45). I come against every spirit that is causing Coats' disease, blindness, torn retinas, clouding of the eye, vascular diseases, and glaucoma: let the fire of the Holy Ghost consume every spiritual disorder operating in my life, in the name of Jesus.

46). For every satyr (goat spirit) that has wreaked havoc on the body of Christ, let the hammer of the Lord crush you and your throne into pieces. Let your power over us be impotent and powerless, in the name of Jesus (Isa. 13:21).

47). Let every benighted spirit that causes us to be ignorant be banished from our lives. Today, let the eyes of our understanding be enlightened, in the name of Jesus.

48). For the scales that have been placed upon our eyes that are prohibiting us from seeing the fullness of who Christ is, today, I blot out the enemies' spells and make them inconsequential, in the name of Jesus.

49). I come against every python spirit that has swallowed families and churches whole so they cough them out, in the name of Jesus.

50). Let every satanic and demonic poacher trespassing and stealing from our lives receive the arrows of fire and die, in the name of Jesus.

51). Let every spirit of procrastination that has been active in my bloodline, that has made me and my forefather miss our divine opportunities and deadlines, I charge you today; with the blood of Jesus, I cancel and terminate your assignment against us, in the name of Jesus.

THE ARMOR OF GOD

52). Let the powers of lust and persevering that have plagued my bloodline on both sides of my family be uprooted by fire, in the name of Jesus.

53). Let the spirit of death and rigamortis coming after my life be consumed by the Holy Ghost, in the name of Jesus.

54). Heavenly Father, let every evil mortician directing plans for me to die, die in my place, in the name of Jesus.

55). For every vulture seeking to feast upon my life, let the spear of the Lord locate your heart and die, in the name of Jesus.

56). Let my enemies that are adversaries of my soul be confounded and consumed, in the name of Jesus.

57). I bind and rebuke every spirit trying to vex me. Cover them with reproach and dishonor as they seek to hurt me, in the name of Jesus.

58). I annihilate every Amalekite spirit that is seeking to kidnap our wives and our children. Today, Father, leave their lives in ruins and make them extinct, in the name of Jesus (1 Sam. 30:2).

59). Father, break the cumbersome spirit affecting my life, in the name of Jesus.

60). For evil gourds that have been planted in my food to kill me off, I reverse your curse. Let the blood of Jesus cleanse me from satanic deposits, in the name of Jesus (2 Kings 4:39-40).

61). Let every adversary of the Lord that is blocking my great and effectual door be broken into pieces, in the name of Jesus (1 Cor. 16:9).

62). Let my enemy's way be dark and slippery and let the angel of the Lord persecute them, in the name of Jesus (Ps. 35:6).

63). Let the demonic networks tailgating my life crash land and die, in the name of Jesus.

65). Let every enemy that has risen up against me be smitten before my face, in the name of Jesus.

Chapter THREE

THE CALL

There is a reason we were all born. No one was born by happenstance or by accident. At times, we naturally assume that other people have been born with a silver spoon in their mouths. From our lens, it appears that they have experienced preferential treatment (**favorable condition**) and everything in their lives is at their beck and call; or, on the other hand, you may have felt as if you were treated wrongly, unfairly, in life. You might feel the hand you were dealt shows the deck was stacked against you, with your life, family, friends, and co-workers opposed to you, and you became a target.

I know we don't like to experience rough spots, or what I consider to be transitional moments that surround our lives, but one thing we can all agree upon is that is the commonality between both worlds: being successful or unsuccessful, being poor or rich. The amazing fact still resounds through our existence: you have life, and God never intended for us to exist in life without knowing our true purposes and plans. Believe it or not, God has a divine plan for you, considering you defied all the odds. You were successful at the place of conception, not birth, for we have learned to maximize our time and energy as embryos. Embryos outgrow the place in which they are planted. We find this truth, scripturally, in Jeremiah 1:5 (NLT):

> I knew you before I formed you in your mother's womb. Before you were born I set you apart and appointed you as my prophet to the nations.

Here in this passage of the Bible, we find that Jeremiah was called to the earth as a prophet. Prophets are kingdom officials, and kingdom officials regulate the king's mandate on the earth. We have misconstrued our position from heaven, though, and made this a title in the church. When we fight to get recognized in the church, heaven moves on to someone that can become the church. God does not need a building to build us. We will only keep fighting to get established because we are looking for others to honor our names, and we work the name but never fulfill our assignments. If your title is more effective in the church than outside of the church, the evidence is resounding that you have not become the church. Kingdom representatives are never about their own agendas or their names. Jesus circulated these words throughout His ministry when He said the Son can do nothing by Himself; He can do only what He sees His Father doing because whatever the Father does the Son also does.

Philippians 2:7 (KJV)

> [7] But made himself of no reputation, and took upon him the form of a servant, and was made in the likeness of men:

Jesus never made a reputation for Himself. Reputations give you the assumption that you have rights, but when you are surrendered unto Jesus, you give up your right and your reputation to be right. We are losing our kingdom representation (citizenship) because of our earthly reputation, and we therefore stay earthbound, even though we are heaven-sent. Through Jeremiah, we see that God elaborately explains this truth of how we became embryos by using His life. God sent you here because He had a need in the earth that went unfulfilled, and your birth is a sign that God will have success. In the first part of the verse, God states, "I knew you before I formed you" (Jer. 1:5 KJV). The word "knew" expresses intimacy through being one, and God's intention was for us to stay one with Him, with one mindset and one heart.

Adam and Eve broke God's heart when they disobeyed Him and separated themselves from Him with their sin. God kept the first thing first; He established the relationship with man first. This is why Matthew 6:33 states, "Seek the Kingdom first." Only when we put God second do we end up behind. If you are a runner in a race and you come in second place, you are behind. We are running, but we remain behind: behind on bills; we can't seem to keep up with our children; we are behind on time; we can't manage our relationships. This is because we forget to keep Him first. I have learned when we keep Him in His place, meaning first, things will stay in place in our lives. The relationship with Him becomes the starting block for us to be released into our assignments. Notice Jeremiah's purpose came before he was ever fashioned in his mother's womb. God established His purpose in your life before the doctors encourage your mother to push. We struggle with this concept because we think that we have our mother and father's DNA, but the real truth is that God gave you His chromosomes.

You are carrying heaven's genetic information hidden within your genes. God hid His next mandate in the earth in a kid by the name of Joseph. In the Strong's Bible, Joseph's name means "God will add." When Joseph was born, the first sign he was heaven-sent was he brought peace to his father's life, Jacob. Jacob was at odds with his father-in-law Laban, and his birth caused his father to change the trajectory of his life.

Genesis 30:25-43 (KJV)

> [25] And it came to pass, when Rachel had born Joseph, that Jacob said unto Laban, Send me away, that I may go unto mine own place, and to my country.

Some people were sent to give their parents their freedom; because of your birth, it will give people the strength to move beyond chaos and give them peace. Joseph was unaware that he was the matrix; he was God's answer that the world (Egypt) and his family would need when the famine came. God used the favor He placed on Joseph's life against the famine that would hit the earth.

God revealed Joseph's true assignment, and your assignment will also bring out your hidden assassins. Oftentimes, God will hide His plan in you while people mistreat you and look over you. Eventually, God would have these people turn to you. Most people desire God to reveal the mysteries of heaven to them, but they don't realize they themselves are the mysteries of heaven. One reason people may struggle with you is because they can't relate to you and whoever they can't relate

The Call

to, they hate. No person in life is ever born without a destiny, but destinies can be detained or delayed by inadequate decisions we make.

One of the attributes of heaven is to establish peace. We can only speak peace and operate in peace when we have a relationship with the Prince of Peace (Isa. 9:6). When God created the heavens and the earth in Genesis chapter one, He tells us the earth was without form and void and darkness was upon the face of the earth and God said, "Let there be light." In the Strong's Concordance, The word "light" means illumination, understanding, and wisdom. The world was formed through the Word, so the world experienced the gospel first. But what does the word "gospel" mean? The Good News. The Word of God is His Son, Jesus Christ, and God brought peace to the world in a chaotic state by releasing His Son. From that release, God brought harmony, and a synonym for the word "harmony" is peace. According to John 8:12, Jesus said, "I am the light of the world," when He revealed the revelation of Himself.

Light was established first then the earth was created, so when we reflect Him, we establish peace in chaotic places. We are light-bearers, and we carry the knowledge of the kingdom. Wherever you find chaos, it is only a reference that there is an absence of Him. One thing we must understand is that callings do not require money, but callings come at a cost; we can't walk into any store and take something with value without paying the cost to obtain it. In order to keep what we receive from heaven, it will cost you everything, such as your obedience. You can measure how much you love yourself by how much you obey God. If God requires you to go on a fast and you delay the request or ignore it, you love yourself more than you love what you will sacrifice for Him. Disobedience is only a place where you desire something to be your way, and your way moves God out of the way. Obedience will require your full commitment, yet we have been taught that we are committed if we just come to church. However, if that is true, if you happen to climb in an oven, does it make you a biscuit? No. What makes biscuits rise is two elements: one is heat and the other is yeast. Without the heat, the yeast will never come into its completed state. When we are fully committed, it does not matter how the enemy applies his heat to our lives; the heat helps us come to the completed state in God.

We don't have yeast in us, but we were born with multiplication, which means that we can increase. However, God cannot release the increase in you if you are not committed. A question that I would like to propose is this: if your character is still the same and you still have a carnal (fleshy) approach to all of your problems, then are you committed? Character and commitment complement one another, and the word "commitment" means the engagement or obligation that restricts freedom of action. God does not need our improper actions or bad attitudes to be spewed upon His people. God's peace convicts the hearts and minds of people that He is trying to convince. However, if we are not converted, then God cannot bring the change He desires because we don't have the temperament to stay calm in a chaotic situation.

Matthew 10:3 (NIV)

> If the home is deserving let your peace rest on it, if not let your peace return to you.

The Call

We live in a society where we have been governed by laws and statues because laws were created for order. Positions were created to uphold these laws. One position that was created to uphold the law was a peace officer, and peace officers have been given the authoritative right to arrest anyone who breaks the law. Peace officers are certified, armed, and specialized in handling dangerous situations. Heaven has positioned us to be peace officers in the earth. God has given us the authority and jurisdictional right in the earth to arrest disrupters of peace, but to release your peace upon an entire house means where there was quarreling between husbands and wives, sisters and brothers, your peace wages war against spirits of confusion and controversy. Where there is peace, there is no divorce; where there is peace, frustration cannot find a place to hide. Believers in Christ are called to leave the residue of God's peace in the homes and the hearts of people in desperate need of God's peace. Jesus gave His disciples His peace. What was He doing? Since we were created from the earth, He was placing peace in the earth; again, He was giving peace feet and a face through people.

We are called to be atmosphere-changers. The acronym that we will use for the word "peace" is:

People
Empowered
Activate
Christ for
Elevation.

Romans 10:14-15 (KJV)

How then shall they call on him in whom they have not believed? And how shall they believe in him of whom they have not heard? And how shall they hear without a preacher?

And how shall they preach, except they be sent? As it is written, how beautiful are the feet of them that preach the gospel of peace, and bring glad tidings of good things!

We truly get a clear understanding of why Jesus washed the twelve apostles' feet. We may view the method of how He washed their feet differently because all throughout the Bible, we find that when there were ordained or positioned people in their respectful places in the kingdom of God, they would anoint their heads with oil, as when kings would knight soldiers with swords. Jesus, however, took an entirely different approach when He washed their feet. Why was this approach necessary? Because He was removing an old order. He took away society's regime and started a new paradigm, as washing their feet was a sign of cleansing them for their assignments. Why would He start with our feet? The feet are the lowest part of the human body. God never intended for us to be headstrong, so the feet are signs of humility and strength.

Think about this for a moment: It wouldn't matter if a soldier had the upper strength to lift one thousand pounds with his arms; he may have died because he never had the ability to move. Mobility is a must for the gospel to be preached. Jesus started with the feet because the feet are the place of stability and strength. Feet give you the ability to stand, the ability to balance all the weight you carry. According to Isaiah 9:6, one of the authoritative characteristics of Jesus was that He was the Prince of Peace. An impartation of His anointing and majesty was released in the apostles' feet. God would never anoint or wash your feet if He didn't intend for you to go somewhere to bring peace and glad tidings.

Pray these prayers for thirty days!

1). Let every evil blacksmith fashioning weapons against me and my family be disengaged from your assignment, in the name of Jesus.

2). For every evil lioness seeking to devour our lives, today I release an ambush of hyenas against you, in the name of Jesus.

3). Let every jackal and wolf that has picked up my scent in the spirit realm lose its senses and receive paralysis, in the name of Jesus,

4). Father, let every parasite trying to feast upon the nourishments of my life receive lightning and commotion, in the name of Jesus.

5). Father, remove the joy of the oppressor from my life, in the name of Jesus.

6). Let every spirit of espionage monitoring my life today be permanently blinded, in the name of Jesus.

7). I decree and declare to every eye of Horus spying against my whereabouts, I put you in derision and confound you today, in the name of Jesus.

8). For every sabotaging spirit looking to obstruct me and destroy my destiny, today, I cripple your powers, in the name of Jesus.

The Call

9). For those that have crafted voodoo dolls against me and my family, I command that the hands and fingers receive a severe case of dupuytren, in the name of Jesus.

10). For every demonic, logistic organization of the occult assigned against me, I send the whirlwind of fire to destroy you and your powers, in the name of Jesus.

11). Father, let those that have gathered against me be scattered and divide their tongues, in the name of Jesus.

12). Let every spirit of heaviness that has come upon my life be consumed by the fire of the Holy Ghost, and I receive the spirit of joy, in the name of Jesus.

13). Father, let every blessing that You have prepared for us in this season manifest. Arrest every hijacking spirit, in the name of Jesus (Dan. 10:13).

14). For the powers of every boasting goliath that has antagonized the church of the living God, today, let the angels of heaven be assembled to torment and destroy you, in the name of Jesus.

15). I bind and rebuke every territorial spirit trying to govern wickedness upon the body of Christ, in the name of Jesus.

16). I demolish and obliterate every evil grand wizard and grand dragon speaking atmospheric curse over my life. I shut you down, in the name of Jesus.

THE ARMOR OF GOD

17). Let every contamination, disease, and disorder in my stomach, intestines, and bowels that has been affecting my colon backfire and be healed, in the name of Jesus.

18). Let every arrow of pollution and sickness fired against my life wither up, and let the hand of the Lord break and dismantle every evil archer sent against me, in the name of Jesus.

19). Let every garment of poverty resting upon me and operating in my life be consumed by fire and burn to ashes, in the name of Jesus.

20). Let every gargantuan spirit covering our region be spoiled and brought to shame, in the name of Jesus.

21). Father, blow into smithereens every demonic gatekeeper and doorkeeper desiring my soul, in the name of Jesus.

22). I annihilate every satanic prophecy that has been spoken against our lives and careers, in the name of Jesus.

23). Let every familiar spirit coming from the grave to deceive me be bound with chains and fetters of iron and released unto the abyss until Judgment Day, in the name of Jesus.

24). I bind and rebuke every grave-digging spirit. For the grave that has been dug for me, let them fall into their graves, in the name of Jesus.

25). For every grim reaper spirit that is seeking to bring death upon my life, let your instruments of destruction become your own casualty. I shall not die but live and declare the work of the Lord, in the name of Jesus.

Chapter FOUR
CONFIDENCE

I believe that this is one word, if understood, is so powerful that the entire existence of heaven is released and revealed through persons carrying the weight of this word. Words never exist without a meaning. Destinies are obtained or lost when people don't have an accurate understanding of the word they received. Let's find out the definition of the word "confidence" in the Greek translation in the Strong's Concordance; it means full assurance, fully persuaded, convinced. Incompetence is what kills intuitiveness. Hesitation means you have contemplated, and contemplation is only a result of a moment when we have doubted God. Doubting is only a sign of us becoming lukewarm, and the longer we doubt, the cooler we become. God has set each believer on temperature control, and that temperature governs our relationship with God.

When a lukewarm temperature is reached, God spews us out of His mouth, which is a sign of rejection. Satan understands rejection because he was kicked out of heaven by God, and this is where Satan desires for us to be — outside of God, so that Satan may finish us off. When that takes place, we become statues. Statues are monuments that are positioned in a place to stay, so when doubt stays within our hearts, we stay bound. We become monuments that eventually decay.

In Rome, Italy, there is a coliseum that still exists and has become a tourist attraction that people visit every day. The only problem with the coliseum is that it is a great artifact but also a ruin. Ruin means run-down, and it is deteriorating. These are questions we should ask when we do a self-inventory: Have we become artifacts? Are people visiting us on a daily basis, yet our greatness has withered away? Have we become ruined because of our doubt? Satan desires for us to be outside of God so that he may finish us off. The root word of confidence is the word "confide," so what gives us this full assurance that He will not fail us? Because we confide in Him, and in return, He confides in us. Confidence is not something that is coincidental, as things never happen by chance. The word "confidence" is synonymous for the word "faith," according to Hebrews 11:3 (KJV), which says that by faith the worlds were framed by the Word of God, so that the things which are seen were not made of things which are visible.

We live in a world that was established by confidence **(faith)**, if the worlds were created by faith. When God created us and breathed into us, we became living, actively moving beings, but what did He use to form us? The land; the earth maintained its faith, and so did the soil. When He fashioned us, He covered us with the soil that He called to bring forth by faith. We were soiled with faith. In Romans 12:3 (WEB), the latter part of the verse states that God has appointed to each person a measure of faith. True confidence (faith) brings the Existed One, Yahweh, the external God, into our existence, our hearts, minds, and spirits. God existed before there was anyone to believe Him.

In Daniel chapter three, the three Hebrew boys, Shadrach, Meshach, and Abednego, had confidence in the God they served. They took a stand when everyone else bowed down to a statue of the king of Babylon. Their confidence was incomparable, as this is one of the only times where you will see a king intimidated by kids. The king selected his most prestigious soldiers to bind them and push them into a fiery furnace, but in their greatest dilemma, they never worried or responded out of their flesh; they lived by their faith. Over time, I have experienced that when I desire to develop my body, I have to exercise and the more I exercise, the more I become developed. What I have learned spiritually is that your faith needs to be exercised too, and the more you use it, the more developed you become in your faith. Their confidence in God moved Him, and He caught them when they pushed them into the furnace. He was awaiting them with open arms in the furnace. God is drawn to faith, for faith is the magnet that will connect you to God. Magnets only attract similar substances. Faith is the substance that is the commonality with God; faith becomes the thread that holds the relationship together, so what are you attracting? You can only attract what you expect!

You will never put your hope, faith, and trust in God and have Him fail you. Oftentimes, our faith in Him fails before He reveals what He has already finished in us. Everything that God does in our present time is catching up with what God released before time. God is a military strategist; He does not start anything He has not finished. God does not have to figure out who you are or what you shall become, because He knew before you were born. God explained to Samson's mother the same thing in Judges 13:3-5 (KJV):

> And the angel of the LORD appeared unto the woman, and said unto her, Behold now, thou art barren, and bearest not: but thou shalt conceive, and bear a son.

> Now therefore beware, I pray thee, and drink not wine nor strong drink, and eat not any unclean thing:

> For, lo, thou shalt conceive, and bear a son; and no razor shall come on his head: for the child shall be a Nazarite unto God from the womb: and he shall begin to deliver Israel out of the hand of the Philistines.

Everything that God expressed to Samson's mother was in past tense, for God was revealing her son's purpose in detail. No razor was to cut his hair; he would be a Nazarite. Nazarite, in essence, was a person who had to live a holy lifestyle where they were called to abstain and consecrate their lives from intoxicating liquors, raisins, and grapes. But Samson would be a deliverer of Israel and destroy God's enemies, the Philistines, and judge Israel. God never left out any details, for in Him revealing her son's destiny, He revealed her own. Her purpose was to bring Samson into the earth realm. God needed someone He could trust not just to release His plan, but to give Israel their answer against their enemy. According to the Strong's Concordance, Samson's name means "sun." In the book of Genesis, when God created the heavens and earth, on the fourth day, God created the sun. The sun was the greater light; it was assigned to rule the day. Samson's life was a sign that he was the light of that generation.

The sun holds solar systems together, for the sun produces more energy, life, light, and heat than all of mankind's mechanisms. If the sun happened to move from where it is positioned, catastrophic events would take place. Samson was there to hold God's system in place on the earth. He was the source that God had chosen to bring life, light, and heat (friction) between the Philistines and God's chosen people. If Samson would not have been in place, catastrophic events would have continued to happen to the Israelites. Before Samson was born, God made a statement to his mother in Judges 13:7 (KJB):

> But he said unto me, Behold, thou shalt conceive, and bear a son; and drink no wine nor strong drink, neither eat any unclean thing: for the child shall be a Nazarite to God from the womb to the day of his death.

God hid a truth about Samson's life in this verse. The secret is once God makes a statement about a person's life, He does not change His declaration about it. Samson made plenty of errors throughout the course of his life: he ate unclean things, he allowed his hair to be cut, and lost his eyesight. But when he came to the last moments of his life, he reflected Christ and decided to give up his. When he lost his sight, he understood God's vision. Sometimes things must transpire in our lives before we see the life that God has intended for us to live. What was the secret God said before Samson even had life? That he would be a Nazarite, set apart from the womb until his death. God only saw Samson as holy, regardless of the mistakes he made. Samson may have changed his mind about living for

God completely, and operated with a pompous attitude, but God never changed His mind. With us, what God thinks about us and our lives is more important than our mistakes.

There are similarities between Jesus and Samson. They both had supernatural strength, for their strength came from the Holy Spirit. When a lion roared against Samson, the Bible said the spirit of the Lord came upon him to deal with his adversary, the lion (Judg. 14:6 KJV).When Jesus was baptized in the Jordan River, the spirit of the Lord came upon Him like a dove to deal with what the Bible depicts in 1 Peter 5:8. In the latter part of the verse, it says that Satan prowls around like a roaring lion seeking someone he can devour. Samson said, "Give me the strength to take out my enemies one last time" (Judg. 16:28 NIV). Samson's hands were stretched between two pillars, with one hand in the east position and the other hand in the west position. If you recall, when Jesus was on the cross, His hands were in the same position, and they both had to push past the pain, push past the shame, to experience God's victory.

Samson killed more Philistines in his death than in his life; Jesus, at His death, took the keys to hell and death. Jesus and Samson both gave up their lives in faith. Faith will always yield a return, because return is just the evidence that your faith existed. There are storehouses where the only thing that opens and releases blessing is your confidence (faith). Faith supersedes time and matter. People of faith can go through the depths of time to bring what they need into their present timing. According to Romans 4:17, faith calls into existence those things that do not exist: the universe, your environment. The elements respond to faith, as faith has a boomerang effect. If we are soldiers in the army of the Lord, the only way we can stand with the shield of faith is in faith. Your faith will become the shield that you will need to block every deceptive device, fiery dart, and dagger of your enemy. A question you may need to ask yourself is are you dressed for the battle? The battle has never been over your house, car, children, marriage, or finances: it has always been over your faith. Your faith will stand when everything else will fail, so use your shield today against schemes of the devil.

Pray these prayers fervently!

1). Father, let every evil witch doctor releasing legionella into the atmosphere and environment in homes and schools of Christians, causing curses, meet their fate now, in the name of Jesus.

2). Let the round table that the disciples and leaders of Wicca have gathered against me, conspiring spells through the air, water, earth, fire, and the spirit, be dismantled and divide their tongues and destroy their unions indefinitely, in the name of Jesus.

3). Let every goblin that has been assigned to my life, trying to pollute me in my dreams, receive lightning and thunder, in the name of Jesus.

4). Father, release the angels of the Lord to destroy the sons of terror, in the name of Jesus.

5). Father, I thank You today for paralyzing our enemies and repaying them that hate me to their faces, in the name of Jesus.

6). Let all ungodly rulers and evil counselors stacked against my life and family buckle where their joints and loins are, in the name of Jesus.

7). Let every spirit of Herod that has been harassing my life be struck down and eaten by worms, in the name of Jesus (Acts 12:23).

8). Let my enemies be as chaff before the wind and let the angels of the Lord drive them away, in the name of Jesus (Ps. 35:5).

9). Father, cut our enemies down like grass and let them wither as the green herbs, in the name of Jesus (Ps. 37:1).

10). We hew in pieces the king of the stronghold affecting my destiny, in the name of Jesus.

11). For the spirit of Laban trying to hold me and my family hostage with hard labor, I break the evil cycle of demonic taskmasters over my life, covered my enemies with disgrace and dishonor, in the name of Jesus (Gen. 29:17).

12). Let the spirt of Agag that has made women in the church childless be cut down with the sword of the Lord, in the name of Jesus (1 Sam. 15:33).

13). I bind and rebuke every gossiping and tale-bearing spirit, in the name of Jesus (Prov. 11:13).

14). Let the wickedness of the wicked come to an end and give us hind feet that we may walk upon our high places, in the name of Jesus (Ps. 7:9).

15). I bind and rebuke accidental and incidental spirits surrounding my life, in the name of Jesus.

THE ARMOR OF GOD

16). Let every evil ruler taking counsel against me break his or her bands and cast his or her cords away from us, in the name of Jesus (Ps. 2:3).

17). Let the evil slay the wicked and they that hate the righteous be desolate, in the name of Jesus (Ps. 34:21).

18). Let every secret and hidden enemy lurking in darkness come out of its hiding place and be consumed by the fire of God, in the name of Jesus.

19). Let the anvil of the Lord fall on all my adversaries, in the name of Jesus.

20). I destroy all demonic cobwebs in my life, in the name of Jesus.

21). God, arise and let all our enemies be scattered. Let them that hate us flee before us, in the name of Jesus (Ps. 68:1).

22). Father, let all the workers of iniquities be scattered. Our horn shall be exalted. Anoint us with fresh oil, in the name of Jesus (Ps. 92:10).

23). Let Your secrets and mysteries of the kingdom be revealed unto us, in the name of Jesus.

24). Send out Your arrows and scatter them and Your lightening and discomfort our opposition, in the name of Jesus (Ps. 144:6).

Confidence

25). Break our enemies with the rod of iron and dash them into pieces, like a potter's vessel, in the name of Jesus (Ps. 2:9).

26). Father, I thank You that You are our light and salvation. Let the powers of darkness be eradicated, in the name of Jesus (Ps. 27:1).

27). Let every booby trap set by the fouler fail and malfunction, in the name of Jesus (Ps. 91:3).

28). I destroy all night-caters, night-raiders, night-invaders with the blood of Jesus.

29). Let every spirit of pestilence that traffics in darkness receive chaos and confusion, in the name of Jesus (Ps. 91:6).

30). I cancel all destruction sent against me by the waster waiting for me, at noon day, in the name of Jesus (Ps. 91:6).

31). Father, let my eyes behold and see the reward of the wicked. Let our foes perish, in the name of Jesus (Ps. 91:8).

32). I release a protective perimeter of the blood of Jesus around me. Evil shall not come around me nor plagues affect me, in the name of Jesus (Ps. 91:10).

33). My feet shall not stumble, neither shall I fall. I shall tread upon serpent and scorpion, in the name of Jesus (Luke 10:19).

THE ARMOR OF GOD

34). Father, spoil all principalities and make a spectacle out of them that want to take my life, in the name of Jesus (Col. 2:15).

35). Today, give me long life and show me Your salvation, in the name of Jesus (Ps. 91:16).

36). Heavenly Father, restore health unto me and heal me of all of my wounds, in the name of Jesus (Jer. 30:17).

37). Let the adversaries of the Lord be broken into pieces, in the name of Jesus (1 Sam. 2:10).

38). Father, let every witch that has reared her head up at us perish. Suffer their colony not to live, in the name of Jesus (Exod. 22:18).

40). Heavenly Father, give me rest from my adversities and increase our greatness and comfort me on every side, in the name of Jesus (Ps. 71:21).

41). Bring upon them their own iniquity and cut them off in their wickedness, in the name of Jesus (Ps. 94:13).

42). For every evil power that is calling me, answer my enemies and take vengeance against them that have crafted inventions against me, in the name of Jesus.

43). Father, destroy the wicked of the land swiftly, in the name of Jesus.

44). Redeem our lives from destruction and satisfy our mouths with good things, and destroy every thief in our lives, in the name of Jesus (Ps. 103:4).

45). Send Your Word and deliver us from today's destruction, in the name of Jesus (Ps. 107:20).

46). I condemn every satanic workshop, and let the blueprints that have been drawn for my life catch fire, in the name of Jesus.

47). I break and destroy every curse, incantation, and enchantment spoken against my health, in the name of Jesus.

48). I break every wizard gate of brass and cut every witchcraft confinement in pieces, in the name of Jesus (Ps. 107:16).

49). Let the enemies that have come before me flee before me seven different ways, in the name of Jesus (Deut. 28:7).

50). Smite my enemies upon their cheekbones, in the name of Jesus (Ps. 3:7).

51). Wound the hairy scalp of the enemy attacking my life, in the name of Jesus (Ps. 68:21).

52). I use the weaponry of Goliath fighting against me this day. I cut your head off with your sword, in the name of Jesus (1 Sam. 17: 51).

53). Pour out Your indignation upon them and let Your rightful anger take hold upon them, in the name of Jesus (Ps. 69:24).

54). Remove every garment of heaviness and give us a garment of praise, in the name of Jesus (Isa. 61:3).

55). Destroy every covenant that my ancestor made with the spirit of mammon, in the name of Jesus.

56). Let every vulture that seeks to steal my harvest die, in the name of Jesus (Gen. 15:11).

57) Just as You did for Jehoshaphat, send ambushes into the camp of the enemy, in the name of Jesus (2 Chron. 20:22).

58). Father, give us the secrets and the mysteries of our forefather lineage that brought a famine upon us, in the name of Jesus (2 Sam. 21:1).

59). Destroy every Midianite and Amalekite spirit that has stolen from our lives. Let our enemies turn on one another and let no one escape, in the name of Jesus (Judg. 7:22).

60). Let this be the season that everything You have written for our lives manifest, in the name of Jesus.

61). Father, let every root work of dark spoken against the foundation of my life and finances backfire, in the name of Jesus.

62). Father, revoke every evil decree and let the powers of wealth come upon from this day forward for us, in the name of Jesus.

63). Let the owner of every python and anaconda that has been released against me squeeze the life out of its sender and let them both die, in the name Jesus.

64). Let the dark clouds brewing over the atmosphere around me be dispersed, in the name of Jesus.

65). I bind and rebuke every stupor spirit trying to function in my life, in the name of Jesus.

66). Break the teeth of every flesh-eating barracuda spirit, in the name of Jesus.

67). For sinister spirits from Satan that have gathered against me and my bloodline, let the Holy Spirit consume my enemies with fire, in the name of Jesus (Heb. 12:23).

68). Father, destroy every spirit of treachery seeking to trouble my life and family, in the name of Jesus.

69). I decree and declare that every evil altar of Molek with my children's name and address on it be dismantled, in the name of Jesus (Lev. 18:21).

70). Let all demonic promissory spoken by the wicked against my life dry up and wither to nothingness, in the name of Jesus (1 Kings 19:2).

Chapter FIVE
CONSCIOUSNESS

One of the most essential parts of the armor of God is the helmet of salvation. If you view this from a natural perspective, when there is a war, you will never find a military branch or division that sends their military force into a battle without the necessary equipment to protect themselves or to defend their country. When soldiers are deployed, they understand their positions and assignments. Why? Because they have been informed and trained for how to handle hostile situations and environments. When many of us were deployed from heaven, we were already enlisted in God's army. Your assignment was engrafted in you, which means it was woven into the fabric of your being.

You exist because of what you were called to do, not because of your family, job, children, or house. Many of us are sleeping, meaning we are not coherent or aware of our assignments. Whenever God has a burden, a person is born, and you were born because there was a problem. Many of us didn't know that we are sleeper agents for the kingdom of God. A sleeper agent's responsibility is to co-exist within his or her habitation until given further instruction. Sleeper agents, such as yourself, are given a code name. The code name is "Christian," and under the umbrella, as a Christian, we operate in our military rankings in the kingdom of God. We have apostles, prophets, evangelists, pastors, teachers, sons, and daughters. In chapter one of the book of Jeremiah, God awakens and activates His sleeper agent. He awakens him while he was held captive; He awakens him for war.

Jeremiah 1:4-5 (NIV)

The word of the LORD came to me, saying,

"Before I formed you in the womb I knew[a] you, before you were born I set you apart; I appointed you as a prophet to the nations."

Christians should never forget their assignments or where they came from. We should know and understand that our current location is not permanent. When God releases us into this world, we are not to get so fixated on a temporary place that we fail to comply and listen to the instruction from our permanent place, failing our assignments in the process. We were chosen; God released us out of Him. I know that may be a hard thing to conceptualize. There is an army in heaven; the angels are God's army brigade, His military strike force in heaven. We are His army on the earth. If you ever thought within the context of your mind, the reason you existed here is your sign. You were created to be a freedom fighter. We were sent to set the captives free, overthrowing Satan and his worldly systems. Systems are only governed by mindsets, as said in the book of Romans.

Romans 12:2 (NIV)

> Do not conform to the pattern of this world, but be transformed by the renewing of your mind. Then you will be able to test and approve what God's will is—his good, pleasing and perfect will.

This means that Satan has established a patent on getting the world to think it is intellectual. He arrests their minds through deception. I am not against being intelligent, but intellectualism is limited and based on your understanding, and people cannot live beyond what they cannot understand. This results in emotionalism, where emotionalism is only stimulated by mental hazing (torment). Certain people often fear what they cannot understand (comprehend), so intellectualism makes you function irrationally to where you think that what you know is all that there is to know. Satan makes some people think they are a god, and their knowledge is earthly (fleshly), not spiritual. There is a great difference between the two. The spiritual allows us to tap into the unseen world to explain what we see in the natural world and how the enemy works and moves behind the scenes.

There is a reason why people don't like you; there is reason why people stay sick; there is a reason people never advance in life. In Ephesians 6:17 (KJV) it says:

> And take the helmet of salvation, and the sword of the Spirit, which is the word of God.

The Word here gives us the derivative, that we have the power and access to take the helmet of salvation and place it on.

THE ARMOR OF GOD

Because it is within our reach, the helmet of salvation is a part of our protective covering, but I believe at times we engage in spiritual combat and never take the time to put on our helmet. The enemy of our souls will only strike in the area where he sees it is unprotected and vulnerable. Once he locates that area, he strikes. One severe strike to your head without your helmet on could be lethal, so you take the chance on losing your head. Scripturally, the word "head" represent your authoritative position in the kingdom of God. Over and over again, I have found myself experiencing people in the body of Christ losing their heads—their authoritative rights and positions in the kingdom of God. Why? Because they became complacent, and complacency is the reason why most people become casualties of war and die. Some deaths may occur physically, while others may not be physical deaths, but the horrific thought is that they may be alive but are brain dead. In the medical field, the terminology that is used is "a vegetative state," which represents that the person is unresponsive and incoherent; a word we may all be familiar with is the word "coma."

The stability of your mind will determine the strength of your life, so the helmet of salvation is one of the most essential parts of the armor of God. The helmet of salvation protects critical aspects of every soldier's life. In Scripture, we find the first soldier that God created in His image and likeness was Adam. Adam was the first soldier, according to Exodus 15:3 (KJV):

The Lord is a man of war: the Lord is his name.

Adam was the first man of war, and his armor was impenetrable. There are some people that the enemy will never attempt to fight because of their status in Christ. The reason he stays at bay with these people is not due to their natural vigor, because their strength is useless against the enemy. The reason he stays at bay is because of the image they reflect. I will give you an example of what I am referring to here: The sun carries enough light to cover the entire world; not only does its radiant light eliminate darkness, but the sun's rays release life so that plants have strength to produce. We know this as photosynthesis. We see the moon at night, so where does the light come from? The moon's light illuminates at night and is only a reflection from the sun. Just as the moon benefits from reflecting the sun's light, we are reflectors of Christ. The enemy views us from his perennial vision, and he cannot tell if it is us or Christ. He only emerges out of his hiding place when we make a mistake, for then our image is seen.

Adam's covering was the glory of God, and although he was a created being, he was perfect. Let me explain: Adam's first state was God on the earth; God created him to never be defeated. Why would I say that? Because if Adam reflected God, why would God create a flaw in Adam when there were no flaws or weaknesses in Himself? Adam was created to rule and reign in the earth just as God has that authority in the heavenlies. Adam had the power to put anything in place that stepped out of place. If Adam stayed in place, we see the authority he carried within him, naming the animals and his wife. God gave Adam the authoritative right to rule and lead in his realm.

We talked about the helmet of salvation being one of the body of Christ's greatest commodities, but what is so significant about the helmet of salvation is that it protects the mind. Adam never had a thought of his own, as he had only God's thoughts. Our defeat can only exist within our own intuitiveness. In Genesis 3, we find that Adam invested in knowledge and lost his mind. There is a saying that says a mind is a terrible thing to waste; well, Adam squandered God's mind when he partook of the fruit. He became the fruit he ate, for the fruit was forbidden; he became forbidden, banned. Disobedience will bring destruction.

When Adam ate the fruit, he removed his helmet, and that one act of disobeying God caused a shockwave throughout the earth and every animal. They lost their minds when Adam lost his head. Have you ever heard about or seen a chicken with his head cut off? The body still functions without the head. The body of Christ was now in a state where every man that was born in the earth ran wild because they lost their authoritative right to be the head. They had no attachment to Christ, and it took longer to keep them stable. Don't lose your headship in this battle; stay obedient.

Romans 8:5-6 (KJV)

> [5] For they that are after the flesh do mind the things of the flesh; but they that are after the Spirit the things of the Spirit.

> [6] For to be carnally minded is death; but to be spiritually minded is life and peace.

Not only does the helmet of salvation cover your mind, thoughts, and imagination, but the second thing the helmet protects is your ears. What is so important about your ears? Your ears become one of the gates that will lead to your soul, and according to Scripture, it is the only way that we receive faith.

Consciousness

Romans 10:17 (KJV) says:

So then faith cometh by hearing, and hearing by the word of God.

In chapter two of this book, we discussed how faith becomes the premise to our lives. Faith is the only thing that brings the spirit world into our reality, and the only thing that will please God is faith. We can increase our faith by hearing, but without the helmet of salvation properly in place, if faith can come by hearing, so can fear. Fear comes by hearing, which we find in 1 Samuel 17:23-24 (KJV):

And as he talked with them, behold, there came up the champion, the Philistine of Gath, Goliath by name, out of the armies of the Philistines, and spake according to the same words: and David heard them.

And all the men of Israel, when they saw the man, fled from him, and were sore afraid.

Fear paralyzes you; an entire army was under the auspice of a demonic influence. Fear has a way of pushing God out and keeping Satan in. What was the significance about this crisis? What paralyzed the men of Israel is what they heard and saw. They never saw Goliath's skills or his ability to fight. His voice and stature is what intimidated them. The enemy use their ears against them. In certain environments, we use hearing protection for the decimal noise in our surroundings. This is important, for it protects our hearing. Are you using your proper protective equipment? The helmet of salvation was designed to protect us from the noise of the enemy. When we have the helmet of salvation on, we become impervious to fear.

This elite army of God had on natural armor, which you will find in the same chapter in which a twelve-year-old kid took the responsibility to defeat this giant. But before he experienced victory, the enemy wanted him to experience defeat. David's family discredited him, and even the king himself didn't believe in him. Fear and peanut butter have some of the same similarities; they both spread. Never allow someone who is defeated talk you into being defeated. The present king at that time, Saul by name, wanted David to use his armor. David tried on King Saul's armor and was told to be careful because he tried on Saul's helmet. If he kept Saul's helmet on, it would have given him Saul's thought process.

Saul thought he was defeated because he was intimidated and afraid. However, the Bible is clear when it says the amour did not fit and David took it off (1 Sam. 17:38-39 KJV). I don't know what someone is trying to get you to put on, but if it does not fit you, take it off. Fear does not fit you; defeat does not fit you. David already had everything he needed when he received his anointing in 1 Samuel 16:13 (NIV):

> So Samuel took the horn of oil and anointed him in the presence of his brothers, and from that day on the Spirit of the LORD came powerfully upon David.

Whatever you do, don't allow someone's opinion of you to interfere with your victory. The army could not experience victory because they never had spiritual armor. We naturally assume that we can use things in the natural to try to compensate for the things in the spiritual. Think about this: How do you fight against the enemy of your mind? We often take amphetamines to try to cope with a spiritual reality, for the greatest battle you will ever face is the battle in your mind, and your outward stance exposes your inner belief.

2 Corinthians 10:5 (KJV)

> Casting down imaginations, and every high thing that exalted itself against the knowledge of God, and bringing into captivity every thought to the obedience of Christ;

The battle was over before a sword was even utilized. They were defeated, and their actions dictated it. This is one way the enemy attacks us in life. We hear about how our company or corporation that we work for is downsizing or laying off people. We panic when we hear or experience a doctor's bad reports. We watch television and see a tragic situation that occurred in society. We become traumatized, and the enemy of our souls will use traumatic circumstances for us to panic or go into a frenzy. The danger with fear is that our five senses will stop our faith. Why? Because we internalize what could happen, and internalizing it will only invade our imagination. Our imagination will only give birth to our fear, because our imagination was designed to give birth to the thoughts we establish in our mind.

We know and understand that our imagination is one of the most powerful tools that God has given us. When God desired to create the heavens and the earth, He did it through the power of His imagination. Meditation will bring things into manifestation. We know that fear is not an emotion, according to 2 Timothy 1:7 (NKJV):

> For God has not given us a spirit of fear, but of power and of love and of a sound mind.

If you are operating in fear, it is not something that God has given you. When we receive fear, it has a way of wearing us like a garment, because it exists in our lives and we don't know that it is hiding. The only way we know fear is real is when we have to do something monumental that will require us to step beyond the norm, something that will require faith; that's when you know fear exists. Fear is not an attribute of God, but there are three characteristics God reveals in the passage above that He gives us; one is power. Here, the word "power" means inherent power, as power resides in something by way of virtue or nature. We carry miraculous power that never runs out, for this power overcomes spiritual matters and worldly situations. This is the same power that created us and defeats Satan, our nemesis.

The second thing is love. If we truly understand the power of love, we will know that the love of Christ saved the entire world. The Scripture reference that I will use is astounding when we use it in this context: 1 John 4:18. This verse states that perfect love casts out fear. Jesus did not fear death; we may think that, but it was His love for His father that arrested the fear, the plague, His disciples, and the world. His love contained the discipline that He needed to finish His assignment. Notice the verse says that perfect love casts out fear. The word "casts" gives us the connotation that fear is a demon. The spirit of fear had no grip on Jesus's life, for He had fear in a chokehold and strangled it.

Because of His love and devotion to us, Jesus restored our relationship and our righteousness back to God with perfect love. That means we should walk within the same authority and dominion He did, extending our love, casting out demons, and conquering territory for others to live free within their habitations.

The third thing God bring us into is a sound mind. This phrase here represents delivered, revived, and protected. The phrase "sound mind" also means peace, for peace coupled with faith will always drown out fear. Fear has torment, and torment is just a form of unresolved truth. We have to give God our undivided attention and trust in Him with unwavering faith. Today, can you be honest and truthful with yourself and do a self-inventory? Are you operating out of fear, or is it faith? Your truth will be the result of your reality. We must stay focused, and the acronym that we will use for the word "focus" is:

Faith

Outweighs

Circumstances

Under

Stress.

Pray theses prayers until you see the change you desire!

1). Let every evil Magi conspiring against me be covered with reproach and dishonor, in the name of Jesus.

2). I castrate the powers of every evil necromancer conjuring spirits and spells against me, in the name of Jesus.

3). Father, I thank You that Your enemies shall perish and all the workers of iniquities shall be scattered, in the name of Jesus (Ps. 92:9).

4). Let satanic whirlwinds sent to destroy our children capsize and go back to your senders, in the name of Jesus (Job 1:19

5). Let the boasting spirit of Rabshakeh trying to terrorize me and seize my territory be slain by the angel of the Lord, in the name of Jesus (Isa. 37:4_5).

6). Let the dark powers of Medusa lurking in secret places be exposed. I cut off your head with the sword of the Lord, in the name of Jesus.

7). Let the spear of the Lord destroy every cockatrice that has been sent against me, in the name of Jesus.

8). Father, divide the tongues of every evil deliberator that has gathered against us, in the name of Jesus.

9). Expose every evil diversion coming against me, in the name of Jesus.

10). I destroy by fire and brimstone every perverse, provocative, and homosexual spirit in our communities, schools, and churches, in the name of Jesus (Gen. 19:4-5).

11). I release every held captive from the fetters of demonic strongman in our bloodline, in the name of Jesus.

12). I dethrone every anti-Christ spirit activity in this region and realm, in the name of Jesus.

13). Let the west wind of God blow every evil umbrella in pieces that has covered our churches, in the name of Jesus.

14). Let every secret and hidden Judas operating in our ministries, operating in mammon, fall headlong, in the name of Jesus.

15). Father, destroy every destructive pattern of the spirit of offense that has inhabited our churches and leaders, in the name of Jesus.

16). Wound the head of every evil emperor and destroy his scepter of power over our churches, in the name of Jesus.

17). I decree and declare that every Tower of Babel that is behind satanic visitation in our cities become ashes under our feet, in the name of Jesus (Gen. 11).

THE ARMOR OF GOD

18). Let us operate in the spirit of Gideon and throw down every idol of Baal that has been erected in our church, in the name of Jesus (Judg. 6:25-26).

19). Let the blood of Jesus purge the foundation of our church from evil feet that have stepped in it, in the name of Jesus.

20). Let us operate in the spirit of Nehemiah to restore and rebuild every hedge that has been broken down in our churches, expedient, in the name of Jesus.

21). Father, let the spirit of Cain that kills because of jealousy be banished from our churches, in the name of Jesus.

22). Let every evil monk challenging the church authority be broken, in the name of Jesus.

23). I command every spirit of drought, disaster, and poverty to be consumed by the fire of God, in the name of Jesus.

24). Any ground that the spirit of Korah, Dathan, and Abiram have to stand on against the church, let the ground open and let them receive hell's fire, in the name of Jesus.

25). Heavenly Father, expose, disgrace, and destroy every spirit of Absalom that is after the heart of God's people, in the name of Jesus.

26). Let every evil counsel spoken against our lives be impotent and powerless, in the name of Jesus.

27). Let the charms burnt against me become my enemies' demise, in the name of Jesus.

28). Let the Holy Spirit detox the body of Christ from all the worldly pollution placed in it, in satanic parishioners, in the name of Jesus.

29). Put our enemies in disarray, severing their cords and their connection in our lives, in the name of Jesus.

30). I relinquish my mind, thoughts, and imagination. Let me take on the mind of Christ, in the name of Jesus.

Chapter SIX
THE COMMISSIONING

The word "commission" means authorized or empowerment given to a person or group of people (Webster). In this chapter, we will experience where God allows us access into the kingdom of heaven's arsenal. The sword of the spirit is the only weapon that we will ever need to engage in a battle. The first time we see God using this weapon out of His arsenal is in Genesis 1:1-2 (KJV):

> And the earth was without form, and void; and darkness was upon the face of the deep. And the Spirit of God moved upon the face of the waters.
>
> And God said, Let there be light: and there was light.
>
> And God saw the light, that it was good: and God divided the light from the darkness.

And God called the light Day, and the darkness he called Night. And the evening and the morning were the first day.

When He was creating the heavens and the earth, God waged war against the powers of darkness. Where you find darkness, you will encounter things that are not developed and invalid or worthless. God used the sword of the spirit and said, "Let there be light." The key word is "be," which means to bring into existence (Genesis 1:3). The first day started and went into night, and God took authority over the powers of the terrain to establish His kingdom. The earth only follows the legislation of a kingdom, but heaven has a mandate. The sword of the spirit is His Word; His Word has the ability to cut through darkness to create life and light. When God created Adam, the first thing we can observe from God's conversation is shown in Genesis 1:26 (KJV):

> And God said, Let us make man in our image, after our likeness: and let them have dominion over the fish of the sea, and over the fowl of the air, and over the cattle, and over all the earth, and over every creeping thing that creepeth upon the earth.

Adam was created first from the sword of the spirit. Image does not mean features, as we may have assumed, but God was referencing natural physicality. He was in reference to His character and morals. What we are experiencing now in life, naturally, is only a sign of what had first taken precedence in the spirit realm. The world is not governed by natural laws, but it functions by kingdom principles. The sword of the spirit presents order and places things in their rightful places. Before God created Adam, He made sure that everything was prepared for Adam before he received breath into him in the natural. God is about uniformity. Weapons from the kingdom are not accessible to people who don't have a relationship. If you know anything about natural weapons (guns), you know the gun can be loaded, but if you never release the safety, the very weapon that is assigned to protect you will be worthless.

The relationship we have with God allows us to release the safety in the kingdom to use it to be effective in the kingdom, in the name of Jesus. Where we find a relationship, we will find where God develops us. We've heard the saying that practice makes one perfect. Well, God will never allow you to practice without there being a target. Our problems are no more than targets to heighten our skills. Soldiers going into a battle do so with preparation, for there is danger in not being prepared. Without the right skills, the very sword that is called to protect you could be the very thing to hurt or possibly kill you. The sword of the spirit is the only weapon that we will ever need to engage in a battle. If you think about a weapon in our current era (dispensation), our choice of weapons would not be a sword. We would rather use things that we think would be more effective or relevant than the Word of God, such as guns or tasers.

If you view your battles from a natural perspective, if your weapons of choice were guns, a gun has the propensity to backfire or run out of ammunition. The Word of God never jams, backfires, or runs out of ammunition. Adam was assigned to look and function like God in the earth. God gave Adam dominion, but this dominion was not from the works of his hands. God gave Adam his mind and his language, meaning

THE ARMOR OF GOD

his words. Adam never knew any other vernacular or thought outside of God. Can you imagine if we kept the same dialect and never altered from the language that was given to us or the mind that God gave Adam? When Adam spoke, the heavens and earth and every stratosphere in this galaxy could not tell the difference between him and God: and the reality of it is there were no differences. They were one and the same. Adam carried the same authority and power that God created the world with, through His Word.

God has never changed His format or His ordinance from the beginning of time. God's Word was given to us to create change. It is heaven's preeminence for surpassing opposition, adversities, challenges, and trials. God loves us so much that He entrusted us with one of His most precious possessions, His Word. And as soldiers, or believers, in Christ, we should hold this as a great honor and not waste or handle His Word carelessly. The Word of God is one of our first lines of defense, and God will never have us in a battle without engaging in combat too. God will never throw us in a battle we are not prepared for. He has given us a trainer; His name is the Spirit of Truth, but we know Him as the Holy Spirit. Without the Holy Spirit, we will not know how to use our sword effectively. The acronym for "sword" is:

Spiritual
Warfare
Officer
Reigning in
Dominion.

The Commissioning

If you look in 1 Samuel 17:45-47 (NIV), you'll see this:

> David said to the Philistine, "You come against me with sword and spear and javelin, but I come against you in the name of the LORD Almighty, the God of the armies of Israel, whom you have defied. This day the LORD will deliver you into my hands, and I'll strike you down and cut off your head. This very day I will give the carcasses of the Philistine army to the birds and the wild animals, and the whole world will know that there is a God in Israel. All those gathered here will know that it is not by sword or spear that the LORD saves; for the battle is the LORD's, and he will give all of you into our hands."

We naturally assume that David, the anointed king of Israel, defeated Israel's nemesis with just a stone, so we centralize our attention on the stone. But if you look deeper, you will see that David first used the sword of the spirit, and after that, everything in the earth had to coincide with his decree. The wind velocity had to agree with David's decree. It was not his natural skills but his spiritual skills. David located the only place in Goliath where armor was opened, and that would bring him down: his head. Goliath's death was a sign of who David became. David established himself as the head, and in order to take authority over the territory, he had to defeat the strongman. When we use the sword of spirit correctly, we will never miss our enemies or any opportunity or promotion.

There are times when God will check our stewardship, where He will release His Word (His Son) into our care to see how well we will take care of Him. When God wanted to check the stewardship of Adam, He brought the animals to him to see what Adam would name them. Notice the animals never had a form or identity before that, so they had walked the earth for two days. If one day is a thousand years and a thousand years is as one day, the animals walked around for two thousand years without a name. God will stay silent when He desires to hear us speak. Adam was mature, and his words had the ability to change the molecular structure of anything that existed. In Hebrews 4:12 (KJV), it says the Word of God is quick and powerful and shaper than any two-edged sword, piercing even to the dividing asunder of the soul and spirit and of the joints and marrow and is a discerner of thoughts and intent of the heart. We have mistaken our vocabulary for the kingdom's vernacular. Heaven only responds to people that have been good stewards over God's son. This is why there is such a great fight.

How did God know Adam lost his position? The first thing that changed was his language. The kingdom does not function in fear; only demons function in fear, and that is why, according to James 2:19, devils believe and also tremble. Adam had taken on their personality (nature) when they were in the presence of God. He was no longer operating in the spirit of God, but operating in the flesh. The sword of the spirit is ineffective if you are trying to use it in the flesh. God will not allow us to use heaven's weapons for a fleshly battle, and we are trying to use the Word of God in the flesh. We struggle when we don't see the manifestation of God's Word when we speak it in the flesh. Adam lost his authority and could no longer use his sword in the spirit. Satan's approach is to deceive us out of our assignments. Notice when he deceived Eve and they failed, there was no need for another visitation. His job was complete, so he left Adam and Eve defenseless. As a result, we are still fighting a battle that he lost. With each battle we face, there is always generational ramification that will either affect or infect your lineage. When we look throughout the Scriptures, Satan only attacked three people: two were Adam and Eve; the other was a person by the name of Job. In the book of Job, God makes a statement about Job that is astounding:

Job 1:6-8 (AMP)

> Now there was a day when the sons of God (angels) came to present themselves before the [a]LORD, and Satan (adversary, accuser) also came among them. The LORD said to Satan, "From where have you come?" Then Satan answered the LORD, "From roaming around on the earth and from walking around on it." The LORD said to Satan, "Have you considered and reflected on My servant Job? For there is none like him on the earth, a blameless and upright man, one who fears God [with reverence] and abstains from and turns away from evil [because he honors God]."

God placed Job in a category far above anyone else in the earth, and oftentimes, we would love to have a theological debate as to why God allowed Job to be attacked. The truth is hidden in plain sight; one example is how God took personal ownership over Job's life to say he was His servant. Servants serve. We can also view this from a military perspective. When you speak with most people in the military and ask them where they were stationed, they will tell you they served in Kuwait or Afghanistan. Job was sent to the earth and wasn't just born here. When heaven has a burden, servants are birthed, not apostles, prophets, pastors, evangelist, or ministers. The greatest honor given to Job is that he didn't limit himself to a title because he could function at any capacity.

In some instances, church titles stunt your growth, so in this passage, we find the very purpose for Job's existence. He was to be a soldier, not a civilian, as a civilian has no authoritative rights to deal with the injustices on the earth. We never acknowledge Job for his wisdom, for how do we know he had wisdom? He revered God. According to Proverbs 9:10 (KJV), the fear of the Lord is the beginning of wisdom and knowledge of the Holy One is understanding. We lose our reverence because of who is revering us. We cannot stay fixated on our titles and forfeit our purpose.

Job's foundation was sure, and the enemy desires to destroy our foundation. Why? Because the foundation solidifies our lives. In Psalm 11:3, the Bible asks if the foundation is destroyed, what can the righteous do? Satan is a strategist; he is strategic in his approach. His first attack was the cattle (Job 1:14 KJV), but why cattle? Cattle was currency in these times, and this is how they measured a person's wealth. Job sacrificed cattle every morning for his children, just in case they sinned against God in their hearts. This sacrifice also reveals the wisdom of Job, because before there was a scripture written about whatever a man thinks in his heart so is he. Job knew and understood he was fighting with his seed (cattle) for his seeds, his offspring (children). He knew you only become what you think. When Satan stole the cattle through death, he took the sacrifice and everything that dealt with Job's outward worth. When the enemy desires to attack you, he goes after your outward worth: money, cars, home, stocks, bonds; he even attacks the realm of your economy. Then, if that is your driving force, he has the ability to drive you crazy, and eventually, when what's left is your attachment to God, not having it will drive you away from God.

The second approach was to attack Job's children, servants, marriage, and health. With all the attacks on Job's life, Job never use his sword, his words, against the one who gave him the Word. In the same way, the enemy will use your trials so that you will put God on trial and persecute Him. One of the reasons the enemy didn't appreciate Job is hidden in his name. According to the Strong's Concordance, Job's name means "persecuted." His name reveals how blessed he was, but you may ask the question, how so? It is stated in Matthew 5:10 (KJV):

> Blessed are they which are persecuted for righteousness' sake: for theirs is the kingdom of heaven.

Your persecution is only a sign of how blessed you are. Don't allow outward frustration to change your inner belief about God. Satan had faith; his faith was that Job's faith would fail because it appeared Job's life had failed. Satan attacked Job because he naturally assumed Job would lose his faith in God and curse Him to His face. Notice the words that I just expressed: Satan wanted Job to curse God to His face, which tells us that when Job experienced his trials, he was very close to God. In order for someone to curse you to your face, they have to be extremely close to you. God was with Job every step of the way. When God allowed Job's hedge to go down, his trust in God stayed intact. God never gave the order for Satan to stop attacking Job. Job's sword became the protective perimeter that held Satan at bay, and with all of Satan's efforts to get

THE ARMOR OF GOD

Job to self-destruct, Job's faith in God exhausted all of Satan's efforts. He eventually gave up.

Why was Job's life a reflection of Christ? Here's the answer: Satan's desire was to destroy someone on the earth, and Christ used Job's life as a decoy to set everyone else free. Job took the full brunt of everything that Satan had to dish out and became the ultimate sacrifice for his generation. Ask yourself these questions: Do you know the magnitude of your test? Is your test allowing people that couldn't handle this trial to go free? Your life has become the book that people learn from. Real truth lives within the defining moment of our trials. This is when God uncovers the departments of His treasures hidden within us.

Take these prayers serious and don't let up!

1). I cut off the tail of the dragon seeking to sweep deception over this nation, in the name of Jesus (Rev. 12:4

2). Heavenly Father, let the powers of every tannin spirit be its waste land and let its power be impotent, in the name of Jesus.

3). Let every evil throne room of the dragon be dismantled and torn down, in the name of Jesus.

4). Let the angel of the Lord release wormwood against the dragon that is hiding in the waters, in the name of Jesus (Rev. 8:11).

5). Father, by the power of the blood of Jesus, let the source of the dragon's strength begin to deteriorate over your people, in the name of Jesus.

6). I shall tread upon the lion, and the adder and the dragon shall I trample under my feet, in the name of Jesus (Ps. 91:13).

7). Dismantle and strip the dragon of his dominion over this world, in the name of Jesus.

8). Let the dragon that has exalted himself against the Lord God be trampled down, in the name of Jesus.

THE ARMOR OF GOD

9). Hew the dragon into pieces with your double-edged sword, releasing lust and perversion in the church, in the name of Jesus.

10). Overthrow the dragon that is wreaking havoc upon the saints of God, in the name of Jesus (Rev. 12:12).

11). Let your sore and great strong sword slay the dragon in the sea, in the name of Jesus (Isa. 27:1).

12). Father, punish Leviathan, the piercing serpent, even Leviathan, the crooked serpent, in the name of Jesus (Isa. 27:1).

13). Lay hold upon the dragon, that old serpent, and paralyze him, in the name of Jesus (Rev. 20:2).

14). Shut the mouth of the dragon issuing judgments against us; devour them that seek to devour us, in the name of Jesus.

15). Let the dragon be astonished and break the head of Leviathan in pieces, in the name of Jesus (Ps. 74:14

16). Draw out Leviathan with a hook and tie down his tongue with a rope, in the name of Jesus.

17). Release cherubim with a flaming sword of fire, which turns in every direction, to cut the heads and the horns of the dragon that came upon our land, in the name of Jesus (Gen. 3:24)

18). Heavenly Father, dethrone every dragon and destroy his scepter of power, in the name of Jesus.

19). Let every ancestral covenant made with the blaspheming beast speaking curses against God be severed by the battle axe of the Lord, in the name of Jesus (Rev. 13:6

20). Let every seat of jealousy erected in our sanctuary provoking jealousy be torn down and become rubble and ashes, in the name of Jesus (Ezek. 8:3

21). Let the dragon be cast down and devoured and a fire be placed in the midst of him, in the name of Jesus (Ezek. 28:18).

22). Bring every evil alliance the dragon is using against us to open shame and disgrace them, in the name of Jesus.

23). I decree and declare to evil alms and blood money that dragon is using to pollute God's ministers, today, I destroy your evil cords and links, in the name of Jesus.

24). By the power and the blood of Jesus, I cancel every mind-blocking spirit and mind-seducing spirit used by the dragon, in the name of Jesus.

25). I destroy and disrupt and throw down every celestial power erecting idols of dragons in every country, in the name of Jesus.

26). Father, let every cockatrice spirit that came to bite me or kill me die by its devices and poison, in the name of Jesus.

For those who never back down, eventually, the enemy will stand and surrender.

www.ingramcontent.com/pod-product-compliance
Lightning Source LLC
LaVergne TN
LVHW041558281125
826569LV00031B/387